WOODSTOCK AND THE ROYAL PARK

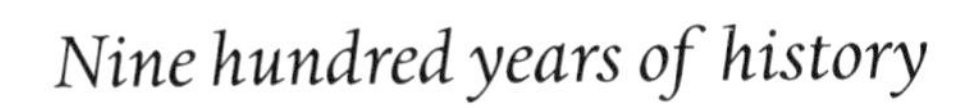

Nine hundred years of history

WOODSTOCK AND THE ROYAL PARK

Nine hundred years of history

EDITED BY

JOHN BANBURY · ROBERT EDWARDS

ELIZABETH POSKITT

ILLUSTRATIONS EDITOR: TIM NUTT

MAP DRAWINGS BY BRENDA CRIPPS

WOODSTOCK AND THE ROYAL PARK
900 YEARS ASSOCIATION
WITH CHRIS ANDREWS PUBLICATIONS LTD

Published by Woodstock and the Royal Park 900 years Association
with Chris Andrews Publications Ltd

First published 2010

ISBN 978-1-906725-40-2

Designed and produced by Bob Elliott and Chris Andrews

Printed in England by 4edge Ltd, Hockley.

FRONT COVER ILLUSTRATIONS

Ancient Palace of Woodstock (*Private collection*)

Part of the Charles II Charter of the Borough of Woodstock (*Oxfordshire Record Office and Woodstock Town Council*)

Document Seal *c.*1640 (*ref:BORA/1/0/4 Oxfordshire Record Office and Woodstock Town Council*)

BACK COVER ILLUSTRATIONS

Map of Oxfordshire by Pieter Van der Aa 1659–1733 (*Private collection*)

Mayor's pendant presented by Duke of Marlborough commemorating Queen Victoria's Diamond Jubilee (*Woodstock Town Council*)

Blenheim Palace.

FOREWORD

by His Grace the Duke of Marlborough

A WEALTH of history surrounds Woodstock and it is a pleasure to introduce this book which now makes so readily and readably available its 900-year-old story. It is a story my cousin and godfather, Sir Winston Churchill, identified and, as always, he found the memorable words in which to express it. He wrote: *'The whole region is rich in history. The antiquity of Woodstock is not measured by a thousand years. Here kings – Saxon, Norman and Plantagenet held their courts . . . it was already a borough when the Doomsday Book was being compiled . . . the tumults of the Civil Wars . . . in the dim backwards of time Roman generals built their villas.'*

The book gives a well-researched account of the great names and events but also interweaves with them a revealing account of how these events affected the lives of ordinary people. The Civil War, for example, had a disastrous effect on the staple trades of the town, especially glove making and bell founding. Under Cromwell's puritanical regime the demand for church bells decreased drastically as churches became simpler. Demand for fine gloves declined as fine needlework was frowned upon, although this essential part of the borough economy did recover – apparently, in 1852 an incredible 7,200 pairs were being produced per week.

The book has great variety of appeal. Throughout there is a serious accuracy of research but occasionally the tone changes. I was amused by the sense of humour of one of the Tudor courtiers of the imprisoned Princess (later Queen) Elizabeth who apparently produced a goat before her Warder, Sir John Bedingfield, claiming that it had been seen talking to her and that he feared Treason lest it was a Welshman in disguise. On the other hand the account of the sombre reality of the impact on a small borough of the two World Wars is moving: over sixty young people gave their lives.

I enjoyed the many references to my family, closely involved with the story of Woodstock for over 300 of its 900 years. I now learn that in 1941 my mother led the Women's Voluntary Service in providing 4,200 meals a month in the Woodstock 'British Restaurant'.

I enjoyed this well-researched, interestingly illustrated and very readable account of our borough and town. I recommend it.

Marlborough.

Contents

LIST OF ILLUSTRATIONS viii

PREFACE xiii

EDITORS' NOTE xv

INTRODUCTION xvii

1 The Normans and the Creation of the Wall 1
JOHN BANBURY & PETER JAY

2 The Plantagenets at Woodstock 12
ELIZABETH POSKITT

3 The Tudors 32
ROBERT EDWARDS

4 The Stuarts, the Civil War and After 43
CHRISTOPHER COOPER, HANNAH COOPER, POPPY LAMBERT & JOHN BANBURY

5 The Coming of the Churchills 56
JOHN BANBURY, MONICA HOLMES-SIEDLE & ELIZABETH POSKITT

6 Woodstock Crafts and Trades 72
JOHN BANBURY & CAROL ANDERSON

7 The End of the Rotten Borough 86
JOHN BANBURY & ELIZABETH POSKITT

8 Woodstock and Blenheim in the Twentieth Century 94
ROBERT EDWARDS

9 The Development of the Natural History of the Park 109
GAVIN BIRD, SHEILA BUDDEN & PAT CRUTCH

10 The Demesne Villages Around the Park 120
JOHN BANBURY & PAT CRUTCH

BIBLIOGRAPHY 143

ACKNOWLEDGEMENTS 147

INDEX 148

List of Illustrations

Borough of New Woodstock Coat of Arms (*The Queen's College Oxford – by permission of Provost and Fellows*) xvii

Akeman Street looking east towards Furze Platt (*Photo: Tim Nutt*) 2

Outline of the Royal Park, Akeman Street & river locations (*Map: Brenda Cripps*) 3

King Ethelred (*Woodstock Broderers: needlework in Woodstock Town Hall*) 4

Ancient oaks in High Park (*Photo: Tim Nutt*) 6

Stone wall surrounding the Park (*Photo: Tim Nutt*) 8

Scene of the enclosed Park to house Henry I's menagerie (*Woodstock Broderers: needlework in Woodstock Town Hall*) 10

Middle Ages – 12th to 15th century. Outline of the first enclosure for the Royal Park (*Map: Brenda Cripps*) 13

Early impression of the Manor House (*plate in the Bodleian Library*) 14

Dr. R. Plot's view of the Manor House across the causeway 1677 (*Engraving: Plot, R. Natural History of Oxfordshire 1677*) 15

Villagers collecting firewood and chopping trees (*Woodcut from Ballard – Henmans LLP*) 16

Fair Rosamund in her bower with an inset of Queen Eleanor (*Woodstock Broderers: needlework in Woodstock Town Hall*) 17

Rosamund's Well today in Blenheim Park (*Photo: Tim Nutt*) 19

New Woodstock Early Development. Street patterns in the town's early development. (*Map: Brenda Cripps*) 21

Consecration of Thomas à Becket as archbishop (*Carved, painted and gilt alabaster: by permission, Victoria & Albert Museum London*) 22

Black Prince in formal dress (*Private collection*) 29

Woodstock Manor House (*Engraving: Ballard A. 1896. Chronicles of the Royal Borough of Woodstock*) 33

The Old Chantry School which became the Grammar School (*Private collection*) 35

A Book of 'Chamberlins Accompts' and the rents of the Borough of New Woodstock (*Oxfordshire Record Office & Woodstock Town Council*) 36

Bull Inn … later called the Angel Inn (*Private collection*) 38

2–8 Park Street today (*Photo: Tim Nutt*) 41

Ship Money writ from Charles I written in Latin in 17th-century chancery script: starts 'Charles by the Grace of God… .' (*Oxfordshire Record Office & Woodstock Town Council*) 45

Payment record for Ship Tax (*Oxfordshire Record Office & Woodstock Town Council*) 45
Plaque to Edmond Hiorne – Park Street (*Photo: Tim Nutt*) 46
William Lenthall MP for Woodstock, Speaker of the House of Commons 1640 (*Painted by unknown artist – The National Portrait Gallery*) 46
Location of the Battles fought in the Civil War with insert of the Manor House under siege (*Woodstock Broderers: needlework in Woodstock Town Hall*) 47
Image of Stuart coin (*Private collection*) 50
Part of the Charles II Charter of the Borough of Woodstock (*Oxfordshire Record Office and Woodstock Town Council*) 51
Privy Council's demand note to deliver a 'brace of fatt bucks' (*Private collection*) 53
Showing the Racecourse and the realigned Southern Boundary (*Map: Brenda Cripps*) 54
Blenheim Park 18th to 21st century – remodelled by Lancelot (Capability) Brown (*Map: Brenda Cripps*) 59
One of the original plans for Woodstock Park with Blenheim House and Garden layouts (*Private collection*) 61
Triumphal Arch, Woodstock Town Gate designed by Nicholas Hawksmoor 1723 (*Photo: Tim Nutt*) 65
View of the formal canal scheme designed by Armstrong (*Engraving: Boydell J. Private collection*). 66
The Cascade at the end of the Lake (*Photo: Tim Nutt*) 68
The New Bridge south of the Cascade designed by William Chambers, 1772/73 (*Photo: Tim Nutt*) 69
'The finest view in England' as expressed by Lord Randolph Spencer Churchill (*Photo: Tim Nutt*) 70
The Bear Hotel, Woodstock where John Byng stayed when passing through the county (*Photo: Tim Nutt*) 71
Images of the crafts and trades for which Woodstock was renowned (*Woodstock Broderers: needlework in Woodstock Town Hall*) 73
Richard Keene's attendance at the Borough Council meeting 1688 (*Oxfordshire Record Office & Woodstock Town Council*) 74
Richard 'KEENE CAST THIS RINGE 1673' for St Peter's Church in Martley (*Photo: Tim Nutt*) 75
The inscription is cast on No.5 bell at St Peter's Church, Martley (*Photo: Tim Nutt*) 76
Polished cut steel jewellery (*Private collection*) 78
Quality of workmanship shown in the detail of this sword guard (*The Oxfordshire Museum, Oxfordshire County Council*) 80

Glove Cutters hard at work – from the left Doug Beckett, Fred Margetts and a 'Chapel man from Charlbury way' (*Private collection*) 82

The pair of gloves presented to Queen Elizabeth I in 1556 on a visit to Oxford (*Ashmolean Museum, Oxford*) 84

Pair of gloves being presented to Queen Elizabeth II by Mayor Alderman C W Banbury on her visit to Woodstock (*Private collection*) 84

Front view of Messrs. Atherton & Clothier Glove Factory on Oxford Street 1923 (*Private collection*) 85

Site plan showing location of Union Workhouse on Hensington Road (*Part Ordnance Survey map – Courtesy of Peter Higginbotham / workhouses.org.uk*) 88

Union Workhouse on Hensington Road built in 1836–1837 (*Oxfordshire County Council photographic archives*) 89

1861 the Duke presented the town with a drinking fountain placed in the wall of the Town Hall (*Photo: Tim Nutt*) 90

Woodstock Volunteer Fire Brigade with their manual pump and bugler 1898 (*Private collection*) 91

Fire Bell attached to the east wall of the Town Hall (*Photo: Tim Nutt*) 92

Prizewinning 1924 Fire Brigade with their Model T Ford Motor Fire Engine with ladders, pumps, hoses and a fire bell to warn of approach (*Private collection*) 93

View of Town Hall, Market Square and Bear Hotel (*Private collection*) 95

Oxfordshire Yeomanry Hospital Corps – South African Campaign (*Private collection*) 97

War Memorial in the Remembrance Garden (*Photo: Tim Nutt*) 99

The 'Fair Rosamund' which conveyed Queen Victoria from Oxford during her visit to Woodstock in 1896 (*Private collection*) 104

The Water Gardens created by the Ninth Duke on the west side of the Palace (*Photo: Chris Andrews*) 106

1947 Mary, Duchess of Marlborough, as Mayor of Woodstock, conferring the Honorary Freedom of Woodstock on Mr. Churchill (*By courtesy of The Duke of Marlborough*) 108

Ancient oak in High Park (*Photo: John Banbury*) 110

Roman snails still found in the Park (*Photo: John Banbury*) 111

Local residents collecting firewood for cooking and heating (*Woodcuts from Ballard – Henmans LLP*) 112

19th-century 'Robin Hood's Elm' in Oxford Street, Woodstock (*Private collection*) 113

Queen Elizabeth's Island with Woodstock skyline in the background (*Photo: Tim Nutt*) 117

Lambs in the Park (*Photo: Tim Nutt*) 118

Snow Geese feeding near Blenheim Lake (*Photo: Tim Nutt*) 119

The Demesne Villages Around the Park: Bladon, Hensington, Hanborough, Combe, Stonesfield, Hordley, Wootton and Old Woodstock (*Map: Brenda Cripps*) 121
Hensington House built in the late 18th century, demolished 1930s (*Private collection*) 123
Bladon looking south from Blenheim Park with the tower of St Martin (*Photo: Tim Nutt*) 125
Combe village as viewed across the cricket pitch (*Photo: Tim Nutt*) 127
Combe Mill today (*Photo: Tim Nutt*) 128
The octagonal spire in Church Hanborough (*Photo: Tim Nutt*) 129
The George & Dragon Inn on the main road through Hanborough (*Photo: Tim Nutt*) 130
Stonesfield Church today (*Photo: Tim Nutt*) 131
Hordley Farm *c.*1900 (© *Images & Voices, Oxfordshire County Council*) 134
Wootton viewed from Top Lane looking north *c.*1900 (*Private collection – Wootton Archives*) 136
This old cottage in Wootton, dated AD IIII, was located below Balliol Farm opposite the present shop (*Private Collection*) 138
Manor Road, Old Woodstock (*Private collection*) 139

COLOUR PLATES (*between pages 62 and 63*)

Remains of Henry II's Palace as it stood in Woodstock Park in 1714 (*Private collection*)
Elizabeth I when Princess (*Painting attributed to William Scrots c.1532 – The Royal Collection ©2010, Her Majesty Queen Elizabeth II*)
Sir Henry Lee – Master of the Game, Parker and Lieutenant of the Park (*Painting by Antonio Moro 1568 – The National Portrait Gallery*)
Sir Thomas Parry – Comptroller of the Household to Princess Elizabeth (*Painting by Hans Holbein – The Royal Collection ©2010, Her Majesty Queen Elizabeth II*)
Front page of the Charles II Charter of the Borough of Woodstock (*Oxfordshire Record Office and Woodstock Town Council*)
High Lodge in 1709 where the Marlboroughs lived while awaiting completion of the east wing in the main building (*Engraving: Boydell J. Private collection*)
Column of Victory with the landscape under construction – looking south back to Blenheim Palace (*Engraving: Boydell J. Private collection*)
A new and accurate plan of Blenheim Palace Gardens, Park and Plantations (*Private collection*)

A 14th-century illustration showing King John riding in the hunt with his dogs (*Illuminated manuscript, De Rege Johanne, 1300–1400. MS Cott. Claud DII, folio 116, British Library – from The National Portrait Gallery History of the Kings and Queens of England by David Williamson*)

The new heronry now well established on Queen Elizabeth's Island (*Photo: John Banbury*)

Bluebells in the glades found in High Park (*Photo: Tim Nutt*)

Woodland fungi found in abundance (*Photo: Tim Nutt*)

Moorhen nest by the lake (*Photo: Tim Nutt*)

Bumble Bees at work (*Photo: Tim Nutt*)

Queen Elizabeth's Island with the original Manor House site on the left and Woodstock Gate on the right (*Photo: Tim Nutt*)

Migratory birds gathering on the timber causeway with New Woodstock in the background (*Photo: Tim Nutt*)

Autumn colours in Woodstock Park (*Photo: Tim Nutt*)

Canada Geese frequent visitors (*Photo: Tim Nutt*)

Clumps of copper beech trees planted by the Ninth Duke just below New Bridge (*Photo: Tim Nutt*)

The Stonesfield Tapestry. 'The vast needlework made by a local resident recording the beautiful tessellated pavement in a Roman villa excavated nearby in the early 18th century' (*Museum of Oxfordshire, Oxford County Council*)

A painting by Turner of Oxford of Wootton village viewed from Top Lane and looking north over West End Ford (*Private collection – Wootton archives*)

View from Old Woodstock, watercolour by the architect John Buckler, 1823 (*Private collection*)

Preface

THIS book celebrates the nine-hundredth anniversary of a stone wall around a royal park. Today we know this Park as the UNESCO World Heritage site of Blenheim and the adjacent town as Woodstock. The royal Manor House has long gone but the Park, although no longer royal, remains. Monarchs from Alfred to Anne owned and walked on this stage and the connections between their lives and Woodstock deserve recognition and record. Time after time events of national significance have happened here.

In discussions about the book we questioned whether to place the emphasis on kings, queens and mistresses or on the local affairs of Woodstock, the Park and the villages. Examining parochial affairs can add to the understanding of national events such as the World Wars and the local evacuee experience in 1939. Our yardstick has been to include those events which we find interesting and which we hope will capture the attention of readers.

We are lucky that there are still many people in the town whose families have lived here for centuries. For them the recent history of Woodstock is the history of their families and to them we can only apologise if there are things we have got wrong. We have tried wherever possible to distinguish historical fact from less well founded stories whilst presenting an enjoyable read.

Many people have had roles in creating this book. Some have contributed through generous support for the idea. Some have given very useful suggestions and comments on the text. Some have gone out of their way to help with illustrations. Without all this help the book would never have been published so, although they are too many for us to name individually, our warmest thanks go to all who have helped in any way. We must particularly acknowledge the help of Oxfordshire County Record Office and Woodstock Town Council in enabling access to the Woodstock Borough Archives and the invaluable support of Rachel Phipps who read and commented on the manuscript using her professional editor's eye. We are also especially grateful for financial support from the Greening Lamborn Trust, West Oxfordshire District Council, the Woodstock Society, Woodstock Special Events Fund, and several individual donors.

JOHN BANBURY
ROBERT EDWARDS
ELIZABETH POSKITT
TIM NUTT

Editors' Note

THROUGHOUT history the Park and its main buildings have undergone changes not only in nature but nomenclature. The initial buildings on the north side of the Glyme probably merited only the term 'Royal Hunting Lodge'. From the Norman period onwards 'Manor House' seems a more appropriate term. Extensive building by subsequent kings led to the term 'the King's Houses' sometimes being used to refer to the royal house at Woodstock. Occasionally it was also the 'Royal Palace' or 'Woodstock Palace'.

A further source of confusion is that the term 'Manor of Woodstock' is sometimes used to refer to the Manor House and at other times used to describe the whole estate of the Park plus the seven demesne villages. We have tried in our own text to restrict 'Manor' to the whole estate and use 'Manor House' for the historic building on the north side of the Glyme.

Once the Churchills come to the area the initial name 'Blenheim Castle' for the new building rapidly turns to 'Blenheim Palace' whilst the ruined building on the other side of the Glyme is the 'Old Manor House'.

For the surrounding estate terms are easier. We refer to the area as 'Woodstock Park', 'the Royal Park' and later 'Blenheim Park' or, more simply, 'the Park'.

We hope readers will be indulgent in accepting these varying names for what are basically two buildings and one Park.

JB, RE, EP

Introduction

PETER JAY

THE idea of the festival Woodstock@900, the incentive for this book, came to me in 2009 while preparing some mayoral remarks for the Woodstock Probus Club annual lunch. Probus had requested that I wore the mayoral chain which dates back many years. I seldom wear the chain and the request made me think about the town coat of arms hanging from the chain: two wild men of the woods, scantily clad, armed with clubs and doing strange things around a tree stump watched by sundry white deer. A note unearthed in the Town Hall papers explained the coat of arms: '*The oak tree, oak leaves, stags' heads and savages are symbolic of the Royal Park of Woodstock which was walled in by Henry I about* AD 1110 *and the tree stump was a badge of Edward III which he used in reference to his royal manor of Woodstock*'. At that point 'a penny dropped': 1110 . . . the Royal Park of Woodstock . . . 899 years and counting . . . a nine-times centenary coming up in 2010 . . . what an excuse for celebrations.

Borough of New Woodstock Coat of Arms 1634

Was there authority for the historic accuracy of these dates? Could they be challenged or just dismissed as idle legends? A little research revealed the source of the information as Edward Marshall's 1873 book *The Early History of Woodstock Manor and Its Environs, in Bladon, Hensington, New Woodstock, Blenheim*. Marshall states '*1110. In this, or in the following year, as has been variously stated the king* [Henry I] *may be supposed to have caused the park at Woodstock to be enclosed with a stone wall. Henry Knighton identifies the year as that in which the king gave his daughter in marriage to the emperor. The park was seven miles in circumference*'.

Marshall scouts the theory advanced by one J. Rous, who wrote a history of the kings of England and died in 1491, that many villages were destroyed to provide materials for walling the park but Marshall also points out that there was no shortage of suitable stones in the district. Such stone walls were *'a characteristic feature of the scenery of the North of Oxfordshire'*. Still under the entry for 1110 and as if in further vindication of the king's social conscience, Marshall cites the statement by Henry of Huntingdon that the king built or improved the town of Old Woodstock, seemingly at the same time as he walled the park and its abode of wild animals. So 2010 is also the 900th anniversary of the founding of Old Woodstock.

Is 1110 also the year in which the king gave his daughter (Matilda / Maud) in marriage to the Holy Roman Emperor? We learn from the Chronicles of the Monastery of Abingdon that the king's daughter was betrothed in 1110 and married in 1114. The phrase 'gave in marriage' in the usage of the time suggests betrothal rather than the wedding ceremony. That at least is the construction of one 'Mr Stevenson' cited by Marshall, who makes the additional comment that Henry Knighton's edition of the Abingdon chronicle dates the engagement as 1119.

Whether 1110 or 1119 (and the former seems more likely), 1110 is upon us and 1119 is a while off. What better time to celebrate than now? So 2010 is the year when Woodstock and neighbouring areas join with our visitors to celebrate nine hundred years of history and association with royalty and with what was a royal park. It is a history full of drama, full of change. It reflects much of the history of the British Isles since the Domesday survey of 1086 first mentioned 'Wodestoch' not as the town, which did not exist, but as a royal deer park. It is the history told in this book.

The Normans and the Creation of the Wall

1

JOHN BANBURY · PETER JAY

BEFORE THE WALL

WOODSTOCK, now Blenheim, Park is at the eastern edge of Wychwood Forest in beautiful rolling countryside just above the confluence of two small rivers. The whole area has been shaped over many centuries by the forces of nature. During the last Ice Age around 15,000 years ago, glaciers scooped the limestone hills into the slopes and valleys through which the rivers Glyme, Evenlode and Windrush now flow on their way to the Thames and the North Sea.

Two thousand years ago the Romans invaded this area in their bid to conquer the tribes threatening their rule over lands north of Rome. To facilitate troop movements they laid out a system of roads on deep foundations surfaced with stone. Apart from allowing the swift movement of their military forces, the roads made it possible for supplies of grain, salt, food and materials of all sorts, including domestic wares such as pottery and personal treasures, to be transported long distances across not only Britain but the Empire.

Probably between AD 200 and 250 the Romans built the military road known as Akeman Street linking their settlement at Alchester, now Bicester, with Corinium or Cirencester. Many Roman artefacts, coins and jewellery have been dug up or found in this area suggesting a significant population. We know there were at least eight substantial Roman villas, some now identified from excavations at Stonesfield, North Leigh, Wilcote and a large farmstead near Campsfield, all within a short distance of Akeman Street. Marshall quotes a reference to a further Roman villa on the site of Woodstock Manor (in the Park) but it could have been at Woodstock Manor Farm, today on the east side of Manor Road in Old

Akeman Street looking east towards Furze Platt

Woodstock, as both these ancient sites are a mere half mile from Akeman Street. The ruins of the Manor House were totally removed in the late 18th Century and the ground level was reduced so no Roman remains are likely to be found to justify this surmise. There have been no archaeological excavations carried out at Manor Farm.

Quite extensive agriculture would have been needed to support the population – Roman and indigenous – and this must have developed out of the scattered farmsteads already existing in the pre-Roman period. The local inhabitants sheltered in round-houses or longhouses and cultivated the surrounding land. They cleared the woodland gradually using slash and burn techniques as still practised in much of the world, to allow subsistence farming. The cleared areas of 'forest' regenerated naturally, grazed by deer and by animals belonging to the individual farmsteads.

At some stage in history a large earthwork, Grim's Ditch sometimes referred to as Grim's Dyke, was constructed perhaps as a boundary marker. It could have been built during the time of Roman occupation although the modern view is that it is an immediately pre-Roman late Iron Age construction. Its purpose remains obscure but the long curving course across Oxfordshire seems to indicate it was a boundary perhaps between tribal areas and may have never been completed. It could be more or less

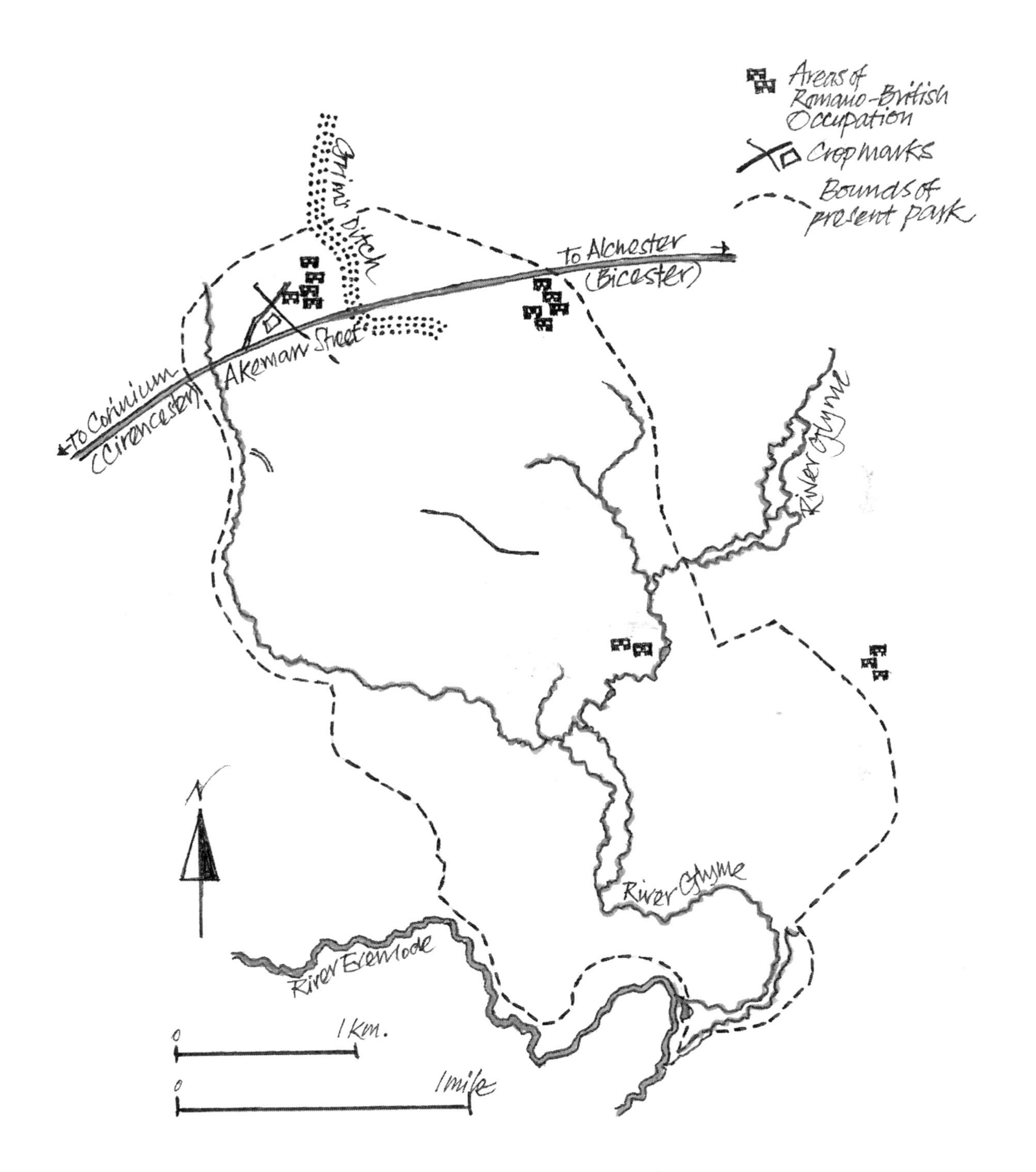

Map 1 Roman Period Outline of the Royal Park, Akeman Street & river locations

contemporary with the Round Castle just south of Bladon which is another earthwork of uncertain nature. Sections of both Akeman Street and Grim's Ditch are visible today crossing one another towards the north end of Blenheim Park.

After the Romans left Britain, centuries passed before the first documents relating to the area were written. Alfred the Great, who ruled the West Saxons between 871 and 901, drove the Vikings out of his kingdom and established a form of 'local government' bringing the quarrelling disparate tribes and families of Mercia together. He was born in Wantage and spent time at the royal lodge at Woodstock. Legend has it that as a child he won what must have been the first British poetry prize – given by his mother. More certainly, he was a scholar, studied in Rome and was known for his translations of Latin texts. Marshall quotes a Professor Bosworth as saying that Alfred translated Boethius' *De Consolatione Philosophiae* in 888 while at Woodstock.

King Ethelred

Even though it was a royal residence, the Manor House accommodation was unlikely to have been more than a timber and thatched structure or perhaps a pole-and-animal-hide tent, re-erected or refurbished on each visit. Blair in *Anglo-Saxon Oxfordshire* has an illustration of the reconstruction of the Anglo Saxon manor house at Cheddar which he states is probably similar to the royal lodge at Woodstock in Ethelred II's time, about one hundred years after Alfred. A long single-storey timber-framed building with thatch or wood shingled roof stands in a wooden stockade with outbuildings of wattle and thatch. At Woodstock the elevated site, the clear flowing water from natural springs, the River Enis (later called the Glyme) stocked with fish and flowing through reeded meadows together with timber and deer from the forest, must have made this a very pleasant place to stay.

Alfred was not the only early king to have had visits to the hunting lodge at Woodstock recorded. King Ethelred II met at least twice with his witan or council at Woodstock during his reign (978–1016). At one meeting in Woodstock the ordinance was passed that *'Christian men and uncondemned be not sold out of the country, especially into a heathen nation and … that those souls perish not that Christ bought with His own life'*. And that *'the ordinance of our lord* [King Ethelred] *and of his witan is, that Christian men for all too little be not condemned to death; but in general let light punishment be decreed for the people's need …'*

The king owned the land. When William of Normandy invaded in 1066, he quickly sent his large army to suppress any resistance. He split his land up into large estates spread the length and breadth of England and gave these estates to his followers. All of these were tenants-in-chief to the king. In return for the reward of land his, predominantly Norman, tenants had to swear loyalty and, when required, provide an appropriate number of knights for military service. He dispersed the estates across England to limit the opportunities for close collaboration and conspiracy amongst his tenant earls and barons. Up to fifty per cent of all cultivated land was held by tenants-in-chief, only two of whom were English barons; about a further thirty per cent by bishops, abbots and other heads of religious houses; and twenty per cent was retained by the King for his own uses, largely hunting and recreation.

Twenty years after the Conquest, in 1086, William ordered an inventory of all his lands in England, now known as the Domesday Book. This would create a complete documentation of the assets held, by whom they were held and the amount of tax each tenant could be called upon to pay. Several of the 'demesne villages' owned by the king are mentioned in the Domesday survey. Woodstock is only mentioned as a royal park not as a settlement. The impression is that the area was sparsely populated even though Marshall quotes Rous writing in 1491 that the Park was '*said to be the first in England which was surrounded with a stone wall, for which it has been suspected many villages were destroyed to provide materials*'.

The land the king retained for hunting was known as 'forest'. This is not as one nowadays regards forest namely thickly planted woodland. It was a legal term which indicated that Forest Law prevailed over these areas and the king would decide your fate if you were unlucky enough to transgress and be caught. Outside the king's forest all would be covered by the Common Law. A 'wood' was a specific term denoting a closely planted area of trees, possibly fenced off to protect the timber from the ravages of deer in the surrounding 'forest'. As today, woods were areas producing timber for ships or building construction, coppicing for fuel or other use and were separate from the hunting and amusement park. Woods as such were mentioned at Wootton and at Woodstock, together with the Forest of Wychwood which included both the forests of Cornbury and Woodstock.

Schumer in *Discovering Wychwood* suggests that the Wychwood area may have been cleared of much of its woodland by pre-Roman and Roman inhabitants but then reverted back to wood and unpastured land over the next 800 years. This may have been because of a fall in population, a change in agriculture or climate change. The evidence for this early clearance seems to be a number of artefacts such as Iron Age barrows buried in what

Ancient oaks in the High Park

was by Norman times deep woodland. Such artefacts would not have been hidden away when they were constructed. Woodstock – that is the Park and lodge – meant 'a place' or 'stockade in the woods'. Wootton – *wood tun* – had a rather similar interpretation of 'a clearing in the woods'.

Forest Law, enforced by the king's bailiffs, was very strict and stipulated severe punishments for those caught offending. All deer belonged to the king and were protected. Woe betide anyone caught harming a deer or poaching a carcass. Punishment was also meted out to those taking other game or wood from the forest. In exchange for living in or near the forest, a serf was expected to provide a great deal of labour within the park. In his *History of Woodstock* Marshall quotes: '*We are indebted for some of the most picturesque trees in our oldest parks to a practice which extensively prevailed of pollarding for 'verte', or firewood, boughs of oak and beech being lopped off for the deer to gnaw the bark, of which they are excessively fond; but no bough was to be cut larger than a buck could turn over with his horns'*. 'Verte' was the greenwood. The serf and his family were expected to cultivate land to provide food for the king's retinue and to forage for acorns which would be sold or used for food for the king's beasts or livestock.

It must be assumed that the forest provided enough deer and game to support the king's court and retinue which, with bishops, abbots and other hangers-on, was of a considerable size. Foresters and keepers of the deer also lived and worked in the area. Deer needed to be retained in the Park for hunting and so some sort of wooden pale fence and soil bank would have been built to stop them wandering too far. These would present an informally defined boundary as a starting point for the king's desire to confine his property. So we return to the stone wall which inspired this book.

BUILDING THE WALL

In 1110 Henry I made the decision to surround his hunting park with a stone wall. Imagine the discomfort and fear that peasants and serfs living nearby experienced when the king's soldiers, bailiffs and servants descended on the forest and started to build walls around what had been a large area of land marked out by mounds, wooden fences and palisades. The King's decision, although clearly recorded in more or less contemporary documents, was unlikely to have been widely publicised and must have been an unpleasant surprise. No other park or forest in Britain had been enclosed by a stone wall. There had been pre-Roman stone buildings, even stone walls in parts of Britain, but the techniques had been largely forgotten during the Anglo Saxon period. There may have been an influx of Norman builders to construct the wall and to conscript serfs and villeins not otherwise fully occupied so as to train them as labourers. Marshall quotes Hole stating that because of the abundance of local stone '*we need not therefore suppose that there was more than the necessary amount of hardship ... attendant upon the formation of so large a park*'. Maybe ... but building something which would remove the people's common rights cannot have had much local support. The object of the wall was of course to keep the deer in and the people out.

When an area of land was 'emparked' or enclosed, people living within the area would be forcibly moved to a settlement outside the park. Henry of Huntingdon suggests this happened with the walling of Woodstock Park. Thus Marshall writes: '*1112–3. Shortly after the time assigned for the formation of the park, in this the thirteenth year of his reign [1100–1135] or in the sixteenth, 1115, as has also been supposed, the king rebuilt the ancient seat at Woodstock.*'

The settlement of Old Woodstock developed around the present site of the old Manor Farm just outside the Park where there may have been a building preceding the construction of the stone-wall. No community is mentioned here in the Domesday Book, compiled before the wall was built, but very shortly afterwards writers are referring to a recognised village which developed before and independently from the town of New Woodstock, created fifty to sixty years later.

CONSTRUCTION OF THE WALL

It is difficult to comprehend how the early wall-builders managed to organise the construction of seven miles of new stone wall around the Royal Park. It required manual labour with loads carried on the backs of men, pack animals or primitive carts. Materials would be collected from the nearest sources: the destroyed hovels of expelled peasants; stones from the surface of any cultivated ground; stone dug up from pits near the run of the proposed wall or from quarries purposely opened locally.

The geological layer of 'upper oolite' limestone is at, or close to, the surface in many parts of the Park. It produces irregular but reasonably sized stones easily shaped with primitive tools. It comes to the surface whenever cultivation takes place so has always been a ready source for the field boundary walling seen all over the Cotswolds. Local farmers used to pay children small amounts to collect stones from the fields and heap them at the edges of the fields for wall repairs during wintertime.

The Park wall had no foundations. Along the line of the wall soil was beaten flat and the largest stones laid on this. Then the first rows of coursed

Stone wall surrounding the Park

stone began to form the wall itself. Probably no mortar was used in the original wall, the stone being laid layer upon coursed layer, both sides laid to a batter or angle, sloping back between five and ten degrees. Spaces between the two faces of the wall were filled with a rubble of smaller stones. A skilled stone-waller would never put down a stone once picked up – there was always a place for it in the wall.

Walls like this could be built to a height of 1.5 to two metres and, if topped with a coping of a harder stone such as Stonesfield slate or an upright 'soldier course', could fend off rain and frost and last for centuries unlike the wooden palings which perished in a decade or so. As no mortar was used, any disturbance beneath the larger foundation stones from rabbits or moles or heave from frost or ground shrinkage would be taken up by a slight movement between the stones and no break would be caused. Most damage would be caused by trees falling on the wall and people stealing the stone for their own use. A Park bailiff and a team of stone wall builders on hand effected repairs hopefully before the deer escaped. At a later date the use of lime mortar was referred to in a document which stated that too many trees were being cut for the purpose of burning limestone to create quick-lime.

THE LIMITS OF THE PARK

We have no exact knowledge of where the original park wall stood but the Park – that is the enclosed area – was smaller than it is today. The royal house was on a bluff at the north western side of the Glyme where the river broadened out, perhaps dammed or held back by a causeway (see p. 14), to form several fishponds or 'stews' before meandering through water meadows and reed beds to join the Evenlode beyond Bladon. The river seems to have formed the southern boundary with the wall possibly running westwards along the top of the elevation on which the house stood since the Glyme is unlikely to have presented an effective boundary to deer and wild animals by itself. Did the wall extend as far north as Akeman Street? The western boundary may have been roughly at the edge of the present Blenheim Park if the New Park section is excluded. In *Blenheim: Landscape for a Palace* Bond points out that there is an area of steep bank and ditch in the western park which could represent the basis of the original boundary. The eastern boundary is thought to have been inside the present Blenheim wall, perhaps running along the high ground to the east of present day Fisheries Cottage. The steep slope with a wall on top would have created a significant boundary. The valley running north from Fisheries Cottage, just inside the wall, may have held a stream. Today, after heavy rains this valley still abounds in small springs. The eastern wall might have been even closer to the royal house as Bond describes an area of possible medieval ridge and furrow, presumed to have been outside the wall, to the west of this valley. Wherever the wall was, the houses of Old Woodstock, considered then as part of Wootton, abutted on the eastern side of the wall. They were likely to have been flimsy wattle and daub with thatched roofs although those familiar with the local land might feel the numerous stones in the fields would have cried out to be used.

THE MENAGERIE

Scene of the enclosed Park to house Henry I's menagerie

There was another reason for building the wall apart from confining the deer. This was to house Henry I's menagerie. William of Malmesbury's *Chronicle of the Kings of England* is quoted, in the entry for 1110, by Marshall

as recording that King Henry '... *was extremely fond of the wonders of distant countries, begging with great delight from foreign kings, lions, leopards, lynxes, or camels, animals which England does not produce. He had a park, called Woodstock, in which he used to foster his favourites of this kind. He had placed there also a creature called a porcupine, sent to him by William of Montpelier*'. He goes on to say that the porcupine came from Africa and had been described previously in Roman texts.

Exactly where in the walled Park the animals were housed is not known. Some time later there was a menagerie at Park Farm within the wall and this could have been where Henry I's animals were first housed. Foreign animals continued to be kept at Woodstock in early medieval times. There is no indication that the animals roamed free. The king's house was inside the wall. Meeting a wandering lion or even the porcupine on the front doorstep would not have attracted visitors and if the wall was built to protect the deer, wandering lions would not have helped in that respect.

In 1252 the animals were transferred to the Tower of London where they stayed until they were moved to Regent's Park in 1835 to form the basis of the London Zoo. Thus the Royal Menagerie, founded by Henry I's inclosure of the Park at Woodstock, evolved into the longest continuously running animal exhibition in the world.

Walling the Park and either rebuilding or renovating the Manor House must have increased human activity both in and around the Park. That there was a significant population of peasants dispersed over the forest for work and also visitors to the area can be gleaned from the fact that in Norman times the curfew bell was introduced to Woodstock, presumably Old Woodstock. 'Curfew' was a corruption of the French 'couvre-feu', covering up the fire to save fuel and prevent the house burning down overnight. Old Woodstock had become a community outside the Park wall, north of the Glyme on the Oxford – Chipping Norton road. It is still there 900 years later.

2 The Plantagenets at Woodstock

ELIZABETH POSKITT

IN 1154, Henry Duke of Normandy and Count of Anjou, ascended the English throne, ushering in the Plantagenet-Angevin dynasty. Grandson of Henry I through Henry's daughter Matilda ('Empress Maud' from her first marriage to the Holy Roman Emperor), Henry II inherited the eponym Plantagenet from the sprig of broom (*planta genista* (L) or *plante à genet* (F)) Henry's father, Geoffrey Count of Anjou, habitually wore in his cap.

The England Henry inherited was a troubled country after the battles between Stephen and Matilda/Maud for the crown, the triumph of Stephen and his subsequent ineffective reign. Matilda was said to have strengthened her castles by all means within her power and these 'castles' included the house in Woodstock Park. The castle mound in Woodstock dating from this time and still present in the 19th century at the north end of what is now Union Street, seems unlikely to have been part of Matilda's fortifications. It would have been across the river and some distance from the royal house. More likely, since the term 'adulterine' is always applied to this structure, it was one of the many illegal castles erected by unruly barons during Stephen's reign. Matilda's efforts to regain the throne failed dismally when she was besieged in Oxford at the end of 1142 although she managed to escape across snowy fields to Abingdon, rendered invisible (so we are told) by her white cloak or – in some versions – white nightgown. This daring episode was dismissed by Henry of Huntingdon as 'a woman's trick'.

REBUILDING THE MANOR HOUSE

The previous chapter described the stone-walling of Woodstock Park and renovation of the old hunting lodge/manor house. Nearly fifty years later,

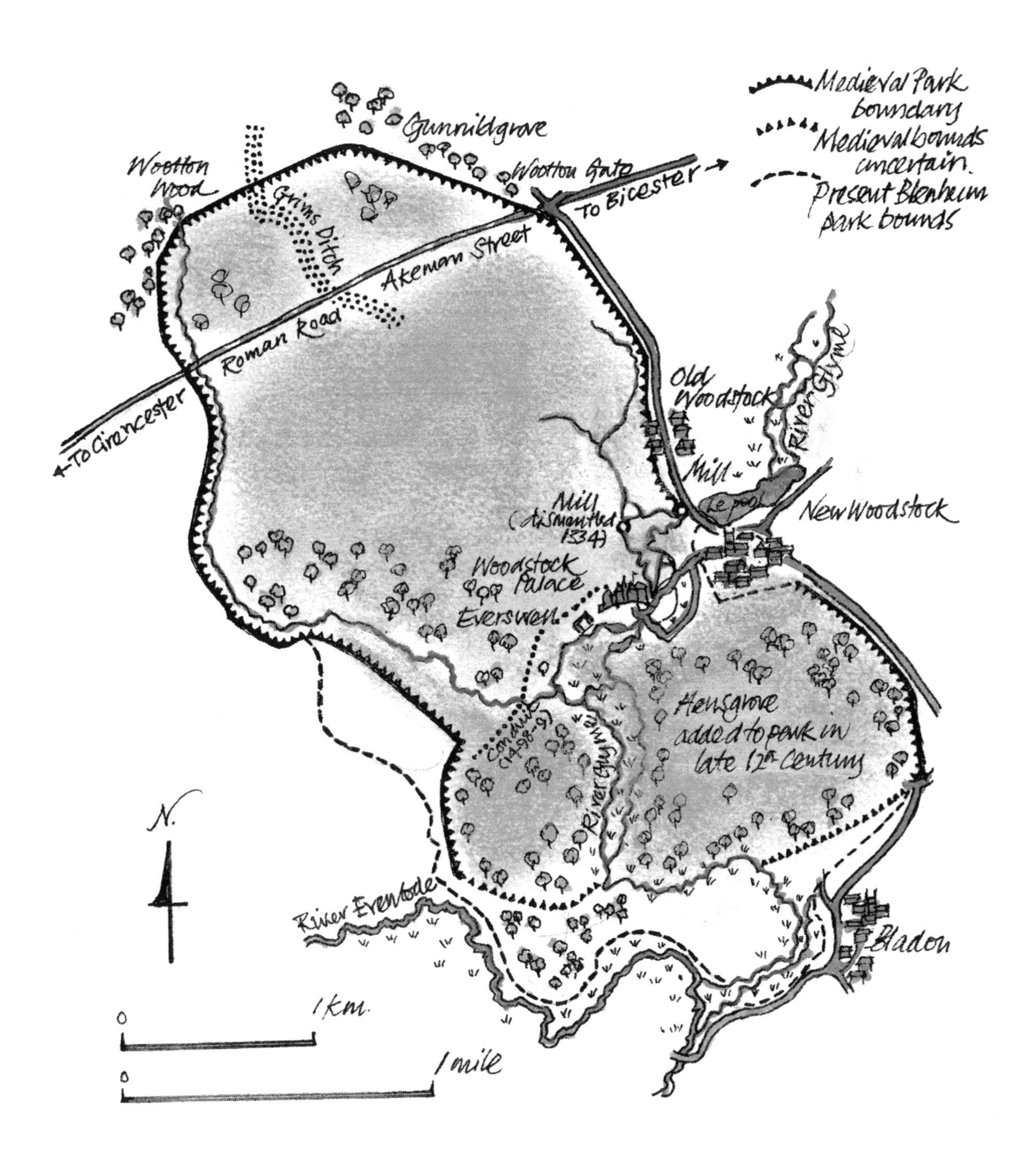

Map 2 Middle Ages – 12th to 15th century Outline of the first enclosure for the Royal Park showing the changing boundaries during medieval times

Early impression of the Manor House

what was the state of the Manor House? The site, across the Glyme from the present Palace, is marked with a stone erected in 1961. Henry I's old Manor House was probably wooden. In 1129–30 forty-seven shillings were spent on shingles and laths for *'covering the king's buildings at Woodstock'*. To the west of this area (and just west of the present Grand Bridge) is a spring, Everswell, which plays a significant role in this story. Disruption in the countryside following Stephen's wars and turbulent reign may have left the house in a parlous state although there would have been a bailiff or keeper living there and caring for the Park and presumably the menagerie, in return for rent or service in kind.

Henry II enjoyed hunting and women and Woodstock provided him pleasurably with opportunities for both. He set about enlarging the house, probably creating an aisled great hall with Romanesque pillars since John Aubrey noted round arches and chevron mouldings amongst the ruins when he visited in the late 17th century. A new chamber was added in 1176 and the chapel was repaired in 1186 when a relation of the King, Ermengard, was married to William the Lion, King of Scotland. That wedding was a major celebration with the couple being married by Baldwin, Archbishop of Canterbury in the king's chapel *'with much splendour'*. Festivities lasted four days. At some point the Manor House incorporated the south eastern section of the Park wall into its own outside walls but this may have been much later.

In the 12th century the Manor House was reached across a causeway coming from the Oxford road and crossing the Glyme on the line of the present island in the middle of Blenheim Lake. Later Lancelot (Capability) Brown would use the middle part of this causeway to create the island. Whether, even before New Woodstock was founded, a second causeway came to the royal house from the east is less clear. Hoskins argues that Dornford Lane running north from New Woodstock dates back at least to the 10th century and provided a Saxon roadway for carts to bring provisions from a royal demesne at the Bartons to the royal house at Woodstock. The name Barton originally meant 'barley farm' but came to mean 'demesne farm' or the lord's farm. If Dornford Lane did connect the king at Woodstock and his farms, the track could have kept south-east of the rivers Dorn and Glyme but would then have turned west beside the Glyme to cross at the northern causeway roughly opposite the present end of Park Street.

The Park in medieval times was not simply for deer and the menagerie. It was busy with other animals and people. Over the years a variety of creatures were reared in the Park. There were fishponds and a dovecote. Henry I kept falcons in the park and there was a stud there until 1360 when the horses were all sold. Wild boar roamed for a short period in the 14th century. There was a continuing need to collect firewood and to chop trees for construction both of the king's buildings and for gifts to religious houses undergoing building works. To help with all this activity, tenants in the demesne villages had to render service by ploughing and hay making at certain times of year, cutting ivy for deer in winter, pollarding trees,

Dr. R. Plot's view of the Manor House across the causeway 1677

Villagers collecting firewood and chopping trees

guarding the house in time of war and cleaning the royal house and royal privies. Tenants could benefit from taking home limited amounts of firewood or from 'pannage' that is being allowed to let their pigs root for acorns and beech mast in the woods in the autumn. Estimates from the Hundred Rolls show at least 600 pigs turned into the Park in the autumn of 1279. The comptroller or bailiff minding the King's House when the court was absent seems to have pastured his cows and oxen in the park and others had similar privileges.

For a period in the Middle Ages there was a mill in the Park. There is also note of a mill, possibly that at the crossing of the Glyme and the Oxford–Chipping Norton road, in the Domesday Book. This would have been outside the Park. The mill in the Park seems to have been just west of the present Fisheries Cottage. It may have been fed from the Glyme directly or from the stream that ran down the now dry neighbouring valley north of Fisheries Cottage. In 1976 traces of the tail race and foundations of a building became apparent as the drought caused the lake level to fall and scorching of the grass clarified disturbances in the land. Even today, light snow can indicate contours of what may have been part of the millstream. In 1334 the mill was removed outside the Park – perhaps close to the other mill – on the king's orders. Did this relate to some enlargement south of the park wall? Or was the king perhaps fed up with the disturbances of a mill so close to his house?

FAIR ROSAMUND

It was around 1165 that Henry II fell in love with Rosamund Clifford. He had stayed with the Cliffords when fighting the Welsh and at some point he brought Rosamund to Woodstock. Henry remained at Woodstock between September 1165 and March 1166 – much longer in one place than usual – perhaps cavorting with Rosamund or, as Weir suggests, refining his plans for legislative change which developed over the next year. As with most of the story of this romance, the truth is lost in legend. Rosamund certainly existed. The liaison between Henry and Rosamund was confirmed more or less a century later by a group of twelve jurymen who swore on oath in 1279 that Henry frequently sojourned in Woodstock '*for love of a certain woman called Rosamund*'. But most of the rest of the tales of Henry and Rosamund are later inventions. How much Henry's wife, Eleanor of Aquitaine, knew of the affair is uncertain. Henry had had plenty of other 'affairs' but it is suggested that Eleanor's last child John was

Fair Rosamund in her bower with an inset of Queen Eleanor

born at Beaumont Palace in Oxford at Christmas 1166, rather than at Woodstock, because of Henry's philandering with Rosamund. The evidence is purely circumstantial.

In the romances Queen Eleanor discovers the liaison by tracing back a thread of silk which either Rosamund drops when running to hide from the Queen in her bower or which unravels when caught in Henry's spur as he leaves her. These episodes are never described by contemporary sources. Just as fictitious are the stories that the Queen poisoned Rosamund or was in some way responsible for her death. Eleanor had been long separated from Henry and effectively under house arrest for some years at the time of Rosamund's death between 1176 and 1178.

In some sources two sons are attributed to this romance but, although Henry was their father, Rosamund is no longer considered their mother. Geoffrey Plantagenet, acknowledged by Henry as an illegitimate son and who benefited by being made Bishop of Lincoln before he was 21 and later Archbishop of York, was nearly as old as Rosamund. He was the child of Ikenai whom Walter Map describes as *'a base born common harlot who stooped to all uncleanness'*. William Langspee/Longsword has relatively recently been shown, by references to his mother in charters he produced, to have been the son of Ida de Toeny, Countess of Norfolk. For reasons unknown, but around the time Henry made his liaison open in 1174, Rosamund retired to Godstow Abbey. She may have been ill and in need of nursing care since she died only a few years later. Hugh, Bishop of Lincoln, visiting Godstow in 1191, was appalled to find Rosamund's tomb before the high altar of the Abbey and covered with tokens of reverence. He ordered the tomb to be removed from the Abbey *'that the Christian religion may not grow into contempt and that other women, warned by her example, may abstain from illicit and adulterous intercourse'*. Despite the saintly Hugh's instructions, Rosamund was reburied close to the nuns' chapter house so they could continue to give her due reverence. As with so much else in this story the tomb has disappeared, destroyed at the Dissolution of the Monasteries.

EVERSWELL

The romance of Rosamund has her living in a bower or a maze at Everswell, the spring to the west of the Manor House. Rosamund's spring or well is still a feature in Blenheim Park. It was here that Henry began a series of buildings from 1155 onwards which were further developed and modified by his successors. There is no contemporary evidence to link

Rosamund's Well today in Blenheim Park

these buildings with Rosamund but Crossley states that Rosamund's chamber was mentioned in the early 13th century as at Everswell and the buildings were later described as Rosamund's. Crossley also states that in the 13th century Everswell was a series of buildings inside an enclosure with chambers for the king and queen as well as for Rosamund, a chapel, cloisters, pools and gardens. Some of these buildings, however, postdated Henry's reign. Today there is still a spring and a few large stones at the lakeside in the area to the west of the Grand Bridge at Blenheim and across the river from the present Palace. The steep escarpment makes it a little difficult to imagine the lay out of the buildings that occupied this site but they would have extended under the present lake. Ruins described by a soldier from Norwich visiting in 1634 included *'strong and strange winding walls'* and a paved knee deep well which he decided was Rosamund's bath. John Aubrey, visiting later that century, drew a series of three linking pools and a courtyard surrounded by a wall with a redoubt at one corner and a path from the site up to the King's Houses. The creation of the lake in the 18th century flooded most of the area but exposure by the retreating lake during the drought of 1976 showed remnants of buildings there. The Everswell spring which still runs today and the pool beneath it would probably have formed the upper of any series of pools.

Much imagination has been used to explain the buildings which occupied this site. The mundane but realistic explanation for the complicated structures at Everswell relates to Henry's Sicilian connections. Henry's Norman relations ruled Sicily; one of his daughters married into the Sicilian royal family; he had a Sicilian almoner and sent priests from Britain to became bishops in Sicily. So the objective, unromantic, conclusion is that Everswell was a water garden or 'Pleasaunce' designed by an architect familiar with the Arabian inspired gardens common in Sicily at that time. A series of interconnecting pools (as drawn in Aubrey's sketch), fountains, rooms and courtyards would have formed an attractive place of relaxation for a visiting court and were probably not solely for Henry's secret liaisons – which Eleanor may have known about and tolerated. Everswell was razed at the beginning of the Civil War. The ruined pools and courtyards and myriad rooms could have given later visitors an impression of the romances' tales of a labyrinth or maze.

THE FOUNDATION OF NEW WOODSTOCK

Frequent visits for hunting and womanising necessitated a court following. Members of the court and servants close to the king would bed down on the floor of the Great Hall at night. Persons peripheral to the court, merchants and others supplying or servicing the court and petitioners, needed to be nearby – and there was no 'nearby'. Henry recognised the importance of accommodation for his courtiers and selected a piece of waste ground on high land to the east of the park as a site on which to encourage a settlement. The term 'waste' does not necessarily indicate useless ground or a rubbish tip. Waste was a term for land that was uncultivated and thus not liable to taxation. The jury who swore on oath in the 13th century about Henry's meetings with Rosamund at Woodstock also swore that *'at that time there was a certain waste place without the said park and manor; and because the men of the said King were lodged too far from the manor house aforesaid, the said Lord the King ... gave and granted divers parcels of land of the said waste place to divers men to build hostelries there for use of the men of the said King'*. The date for 'giving' this land seems unclear. Crossley suggests it may only have been shortly before Henry's death in 1189 since Woodstock is not mentioned as a demesne town in 1177. The mention of 'giving' the land suggests it was the king's land. In 1200 there was argument that the waste land was part of Hensington and owned by the Knights Templar who had been given the land at Hensington by grateful followers

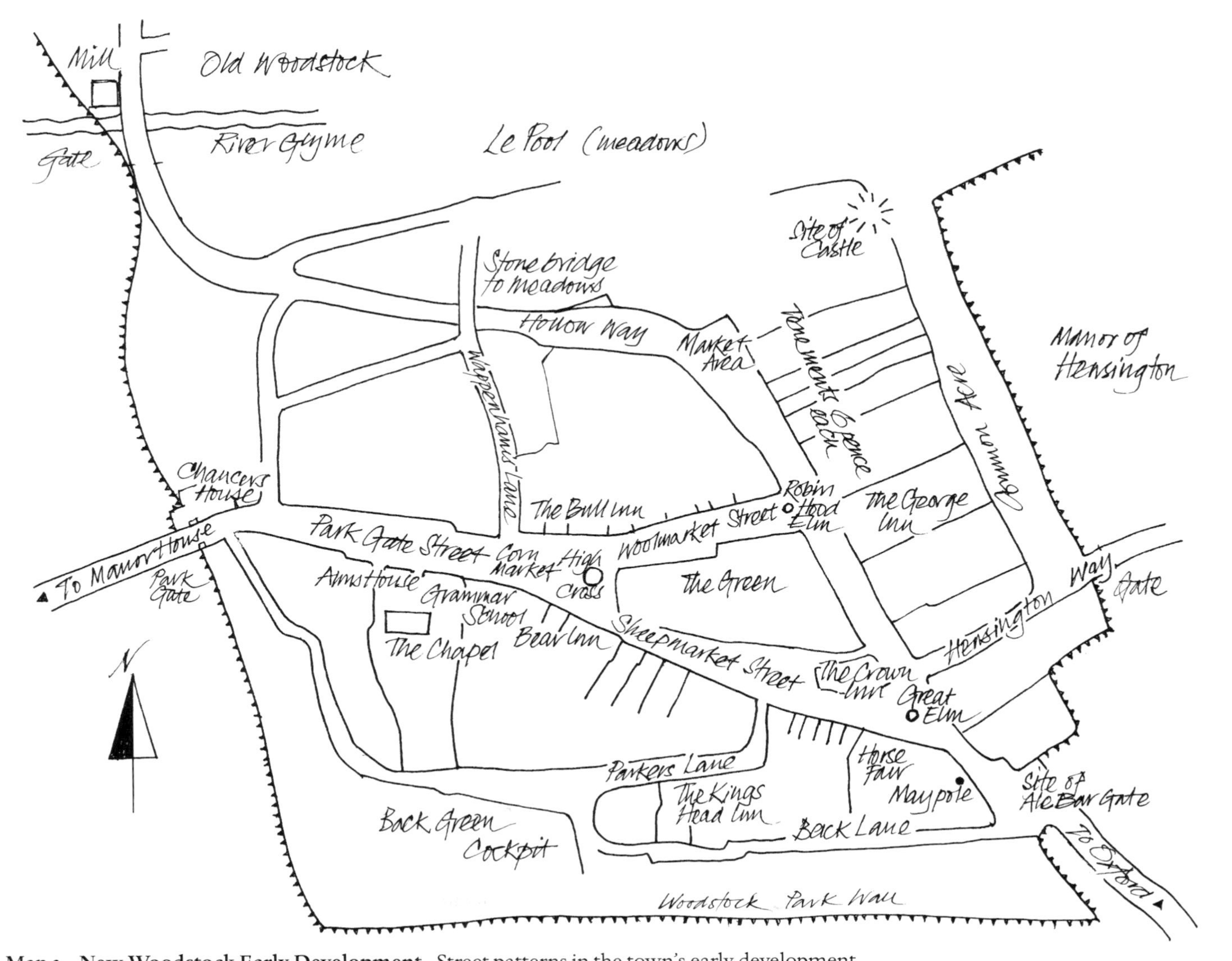

Map 3 New Woodstock Early Development Street patterns in the town's early development
Parkgate Street – Park Street; Sheepmarket Street – High Street; Woolmarket Street – Market Street; Parker's Lane – Park Lane; Common Acre – Union Street; Wappenham's Lane – Brown's Lane; The Green was occupied by the Fell Market, Coppery Market, Wool Barn and later a Horse Fair

of Stephen for services rendered in the wars with Matilda / Maud. It seems very possible that this area – not enclosed by the original stone wall – was in Hensington. The King may have exchanged it for land elsewhere, often said to be at Hordley ... or perhaps he just took it.

The layout of the new town can still be seen in the main part of (New) Woodstock today. The main road ran east to west from the Oxford to Chipping Norton road towards the park gates which were more directly at the end of today's Park Street than today's Blenheim Town Gate. From roughly where today's Town Hall stands to the main road was the Green. Typical medieval town burgage plots were developed at right angles to both sides of the street with the narrow side of each plot facing on to the street. Burgage plots were designed to be long enough to provide sufficient space behind the dwellings for digging successive privy pits in sequence when each in its turn became full.

The structure of long thin plots with some plots now merged into one dwelling site and even some of the back lanes can still be recognised in parts of Woodstock today. This formation is not seen in the area around the present Crown pub as it was developed later when the Green ceased to exist. The original houses were owned by burgesses – freemen who paid rent rather than rendering service in kind to the king. Towns and villages do not only need inhabitants but supplies so Henry gave permission for a market at Woodstock ... and New Woodstock was born.

HENRY II V. FUTURE SAINTS

Consecration of Thomas à Becket as archbishop

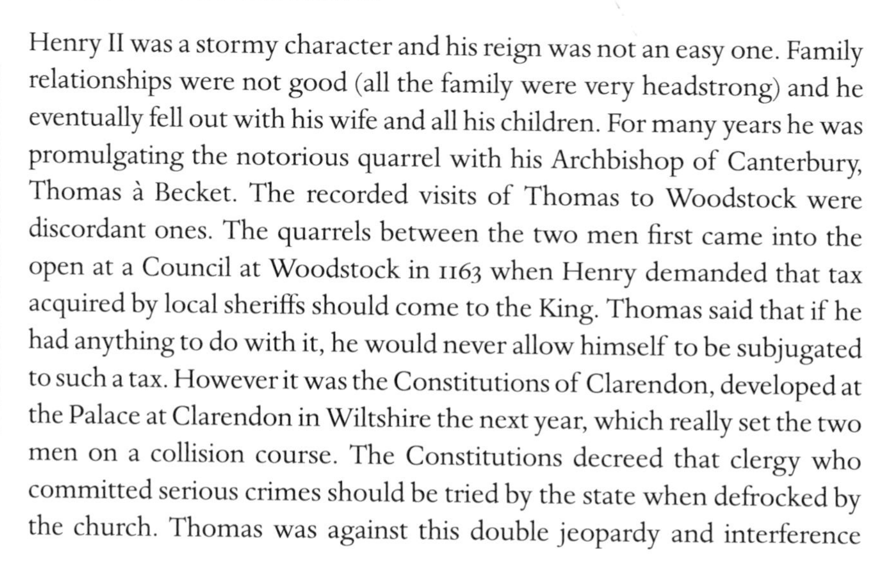

Henry II was a stormy character and his reign was not an easy one. Family relationships were not good (all the family were very headstrong) and he eventually fell out with his wife and all his children. For many years he was promulgating the notorious quarrel with his Archbishop of Canterbury, Thomas à Becket. The recorded visits of Thomas to Woodstock were discordant ones. The quarrels between the two men first came into the open at a Council at Woodstock in 1163 when Henry demanded that tax acquired by local sheriffs should come to the King. Thomas said that if he had anything to do with it, he would never allow himself to be subjugated to such a tax. However it was the Constitutions of Clarendon, developed at the Palace at Clarendon in Wiltshire the next year, which really set the two men on a collision course. The Constitutions decreed that clergy who committed serious crimes should be tried by the state when defrocked by the church. Thomas was against this double jeopardy and interference with Papal control. Making such a fuss over criminal clergy may seem to us a minor affair of state but around thirty thousand people were employed by the church in the early medieval years, perhaps two percent of the adult male population. Arguments, and standoffs brokered by others for the two obstinate men, went on for years whilst the protagonists moved between England and France. On several occasions Thomas came to Woodstock seeking reconciliation. Early on in the quarrel he was summoned to meet a papal legate who persuaded him to acquiesce to the King's demands – which Thomas, reluctantly but only temporarily, did. The next year he went again to Woodstock (was he summoned or did he go voluntarily?) and was confronted by *'the chace of Woodstoke, surrounded with a wall of stone, where he had heard that the king was; but he was repulsed from the door …'*. He then attempted to go into exile but, as he was not allowed to leave the country without the King's permission, the boatman who recognised him quickly brought him back to English shores. Thomas was summoned again to Woodstock and was on this occasion seen by the King and another temporary peace was formed. Despite this the quarrel went on.

According to Marshall, although not substantiated in Barlow's biography of Thomas which places events at Fordingbridge, Woodstock featured in the final stages of the drama. Thomas had returned to England from a six year exile. Henry II was in France. The 'Young King Henry', Henry II's eldest son who had been crowned by the Archbishop of York but against Thomas' wishes so as to confirm him as Henry II's rightful heir, was at Woodstock for the Christmas season of 1170. (The 'Young King' was king in title only. His father remained official sovereign and did not divest any powers in the 'Young King'). Simon, Abbott of St Albans where Thomas was staying and a strong supporter of Thomas, came to Woodstock seeking mediation from the Young King. Sadly he returned empty handed from Woodstock where, Marshall comments *'he found nothing but pride and anger, without effecting the purpose for which he went'*. Days later Thomas was murdered in Canterbury Cathedral.

Thomas à Becket was not the only future saint to feature in Woodstock's history. Woodstock was in the diocese of Lincoln. Hugh, Bishop of Lincoln, is the saint to whom the Roman Catholic church in Woodstock is dedicated and we have already mentioned Hugh and his role in moving Rosamund's tomb at Godstow. Hugh was actually elected Bishop at an eight day Council in Eynsham in 1186. Henry II attended this Council, riding over from Woodstock each day. He was very forceful in his intention of seeing Hugh made Bishop of Lincoln and this swung the vote in favour of one who was an outside candidate. Hugh, on hearing of his appointment and the situation under which he had been elected, refused to accept the bishopric until the canons had voted again, without interference, in their own chapter house at Lincoln. Not surprisingly, given the power of the monarch, the change of venue did not alter the result of the vote.

Henry seems to have made a habit of falling out with future saints. He had introduced strict new Forest Laws which created plenty of opportunities for foresters across the country to mistreat and extort money from hapless peasants. Hugh was so angered by the activities of Godfrey, the King's Chief Forester, that he had him excommunicated and wanted to have him punished physically as well. Henry objected and then tried to resolve the situation with a tit for tat: Hugh should appoint a nominee of the King to a prebendery position in the Cathedral. Hugh refused and was summoned to attend Henry at Woodstock to explain himself. The story goes that when Henry saw Hugh approaching the King's Houses at Woodstock he took his court to a glade in the Park where all sat down. When Hugh arrived at this place he was greeted by a wall of silence and no seat. Gently he pushed aside an earl and sat down close to the King. The silence continued until Henry called for a needle and thread and, pretending to ignore Hugh, started to stitch up a leather bandage on an injured finger. At this Hugh, who was himself from Burgundy in France, made a comment to the effect: *'how like you are to your relatives in Falaise'*. The stories vary at this point as to whether Henry began to roll around in rage or in mirth but, if the former, this rapidly turned to the latter. Explaining the joke to his courtiers he pointed out that his great-grandfather William of Normandy was the bastard son of a tanner's daughter from Falaise, Normandy. The story may have had a further dimension. Douglas's biography of William the Conqueror relates a tale that William, when besieging the town of Alençon, had been taunted by besieged citizens waving hides and skins at him from the city walls.

The Woodstock episode ended happily for all except Godfrey the Forester as Henry allowed Hugh his wish to punish the man with 'a good flogging'. We are told that, like some schoolboys justly punished by their masters, Godfrey was evermore the devoted friend and follower of the future saint.

LATER PLANTAGENETS

Henry II died in 1189. Richard, his second son (the Young King having predeceased his father) succeeded him. Richard spent less than ten months of his ten year reign in England but Marshall reports him as visiting Woodstock in April 1194 shortly after his ransom had been paid. Alison Weir cites Richard as keeping a crocodile at Woodstock but otherwise Richard seems to have had little contact with Woodstock as king. He was succeeded by his brother John who spent a lot of time at Woodstock. Perhaps surprisingly, in view of his callous reputation, John was concerned by the poverty and deprivation of the new town. The poverty may have been a consequence of the dependency of the town on the presence of the court in Woodstock or of the poverty of the country following Richard's crusades and his mother Eleanor's success in extracting ransom from the population of England for her favourite son imprisoned in Austria. Or it may have been a direct result of John's own profligacy. Or a series of poor harvests. Whatever the explanation, John is reputed to have granted Woodstock a three day fair at the Feast of St Matthew (September 21st) although Crossley attributes this St Matthew Fair to Henry III in 1250. A further fair on St Mary Magdalene's day (July 22nd) was granted some time before 1318. Later Henry VI extended permission for the fairs to run for two days on either side of the saints' days.

It may seem odd that a fair would help an impoverished town. Medieval trade was strictly controlled in terms of what an individual could sell, who could sell and where he or she could sell. The market granted by Henry II when he set up New Woodstock was important since it allowed a weekly opportunity for people to come from outside the town to buy and sell items which were not needed every day. Further, some goods were sold wholesale at markets enabling local traders to build up their stocks. Fairs, on the other hand, brought in a much greater variety of goods than markets and allowed people to buy exotic items such as foreign fruits or to buy significant amounts of wholesale goods. Medieval fairs were traditionally set around a saint's day between March and November, spanning three days with a day on either side of the saint's day. Fairs would bring thousands of people into towns but they had their downside as the large numbers of visitors often led to disturbances so that many fairs had special courts attached to them. Local shops often felt obliged to close for security or because the land outside them was taken over by outsiders' stalls – something with reverberations for shops at fair times today.

John was attributed with other good deeds in the town in that he was considered to have founded a chantry dedicated to St Margaret in Woodstock chapel together with some houses and cottages in relation to this and a priest '*to celebrate for his soul*'. Unfortunately for John's reputation this tale of generosity may be incorrect. Ballard comments that the chantry and cottages were recorded by a Report to the Commissioners in the 16th century as the foundation of an Edward Croft. Ballard concludes that perhaps King John was a benefactor to part of the building going on in the chapel at this time so John's contribution may have been no more than a donation to this charity.

The church building at Woodstock has an uncertain origin. A Romanesque door indicates a building perhaps even contemporary with the origins of New Woodstock. The building was however only a chapel of ease of the much older parish of Bladon but John's provision of a priest did mean that townspeople did not have to trail over to Bladon for services. Only in 1686 did the Bishop of Oxford, at his own expense, arrange for accommodation for the Rector of Bladon to be housed in New Woodstock and for the building to be kept in trust by the Mayor and Commonality of Woodstock. As Woodstock was by far the most populous part of the parish this must have helped the priest perform his duties. However the parish remained Bladon *cum* Woodstock until the 21st century when it joined with several other parishes to become the Blenheim Benefice.

Under the long reign of John's son, Henry III, the King's Houses at Woodstock were extensively reconstructed and developed. Henry refurbished apartments and built several new chapels including one for the queen which according to Crossley had an undercroft and crenellated walls. In the thirteenth century the hall and chamber were reached by a great staircase to which a porch with thirty-five stone steps was added in 1231. Around this time too there were two courtyards, a barn near the park gate and stables for the king and queen. In 1240 an exchequer was installed. This seems to have been an actual counting house although there was an order also for what was evidently a chest in which to keep the king's treasure.

Henry's building works may have reflected the event which was nearly his undoing. In 1237, a madman had been following him around Woodstock one day accusing him of usurping the crown and demanding that he hand over the crown. Henry had refused to have the man detained. The madman managed to get into Henry's chamber at night through a window. Luckily, Henry was spending that night in the Queen's chamber.

The story relates that a maid Margaret Biseth (or Biset) was piously reading or singing psalms by candlelight when she was disturbed by a rumpus in the King's chamber where the potential assassin was searching the wardrobes brandishing a knife. She raised the alarm and the man was finally detained. This time the King offered no pardon and the man was punished by being torn limb from limb by horses at Coventry shortly afterwards. It is not entirely clear why this happened at Coventry but it is a relief that such barbarity did not happen in Woodstock. What reward Margaret Biseth received is not specifically stated. However it is suggested that she later founded her own nunnery and the King is reported to have contributed generously to the Biseth family's leper foundation in memory of his Queen Eleanor (of Provence) so perhaps Margaret's bravery was properly recognised.

Henry III continued to use Woodstock for occasional important meetings. In 1247 Llywelyn and David, sons of the deceased Griffith King of North Wales, came to seek clemency. They were made to sign the Treaty of Woodstock and accept vassalage and a commitment to raise 500 men to serve in war alongside the King. This vassalage did not last and Llywelyn sided with Simon de Montfort in the rebellion against Henry and later fought against Edward I. He was killed, possibly through some deceitful ruse, at the battle of Orwain Bridge near Builth against forces led by Edmund Mortimer. A list of co-conspirators was found tucked in his breeches.

This was a time when Woodstock was a popular home for successive kings. Henry III had a very happy reunion with his daughter Margaret of Scotland and her husband Alexander in 1256. Matthew Paris, cited by Marshall, makes it sounds a bit like a sightseeing tour. The Scots, he says, had come '*so that they might consider the manners and customs of the English*'. When the families met Paris describes a truly warm reunion. '*The King of England ... met them with the greatest rejoicing; as they approached, rushed into their embraces and exchanged sweet and familiar converse with them*'. The crowd of guests accompanying the royal families was such that there was no spare accommodation in Oxford or the villages around, let alone in the town of Woodstock or in the King's Houses. After celebrations at Woodstock the party moved on to London but the numbers were so great that they were divided up to travel down different roads to London. Presumably 'hotel' accommodation in London managed to cope.

From early in the 14th century the Woodstock Manor was usually seen as a dowry for the Queen. Edward II seems to have been the first to grant

Woodstock to his Queen – Isabella. In 1326 Queen Isabella was noted as residing at Woodstock *'amidst much gaiety'*. It seems probable that she was with her lover Roger Mortimer as later in the year she went to Oxford with Roger Mortimer *'in pursuance of the King'*. However despite being in the Queen's dowry, Woodstock continued to provide an occasional home for the royal families, particularly for Edward III and his family and for Henry VI. Edward III's first wife, Philippa, was particularly fond of the Manor House, its gardens and the Park. Queen Pool on the Glyme, now the eastern part of the lake, was named for her. We know also that Richard II spent time in Woodstock as there was an incident during the 1389 Christmas festivities at the King's Houses when Richard was present. The highly regarded Earl of Pembroke, who was only learning to joust, received *'an unlucky blow and died of the bruise'*.

ROYAL BIRTHS AT WOODSTOCK

Several royal children were born in the King's Houses. Royal birth at Woodstock was not very propitious. The second son of Edward I, Edmund of Woodstock, was led to believe that his brother Edward II had not died at Berkeley Castle but was still alive and imprisoned at Corfe Castle. Edmund sent letters trying to communicate with his brother. These letters were intercepted and he was accused of treason. Under pressure from his mother and Mortimer, Edmund's nephew Edward III who was not yet eighteen, signed the death warrant. Marshall quotes London as the place of execution but Ian Mortimer in his book *The Perfect King* gives Winchester as the place of execution. Wherever the execution did take place, both writers are clear the usual executioner absented himself from the event. Edmund had to wait on the scaffold clad only in his shirt until evening when a felon was found who would wield the axe in exchange for a pardon. Ian Mortimer in his book on Edward III provides strong evidence that Edward II *was* still alive and went from Corfe to Ireland then Avignon and Italy where he finished his life in a hermitage.

The Black Prince, Edward of Woodstock, and first son of Edward III, was also born in Woodstock but died before inheriting the throne. He is sometimes reported as being born at Praunce's Place in Woodstock but this seems to have been either a misinterpretation of the surname Praunce as Prince or the assumption that Woodstock Manor meant the Manor Farm house in Old Woodstock rather than the King's Houses in the park. If the heir to the throne was to be born in Woodstock, it would have been in the King's Houses. Thomas of Woodstock, another of Edward III's sons and Duke of Gloucester, was smothered with a mattress at Calais apparently on the orders of his nephew Richard II.

Joanna, daughter of Edward III, also born at Woodstock, was initially engaged (aged four) to the heir to the Austrian throne. However she had no sooner reached Austria than her prospective father in law died and the marriage was abandoned. Later she was travelling to Spain to marry the son of the Prince of Castile but died of the plague on her way to the wedding. She may have escaped a miserable marriage as her fiancé later became known as Pedro the Cruel following his treacherous massacre of a delegation of Moors from Granada led by Abu Said who came with his retinue to seek peace. As an aside to our Woodstock story, Pedro stole an egg-sized 'ruby', actually only a large garnet, from the body of Abu Said and it was this ruby which he later gave to the Black Prince in recompense for help in a conflict with his stepbrother. The Black Prince was led to expect the reward of further jewels and hung around waiting for Pedro to produce them. His troops became sick and many died before the Prince abandoned any other reward and returned home. This prolonged sojourn in Spain may have initiated the long illness that finally killed the heir to the English throne. The Black Prince's Ruby was in Henry V's cap at Agincourt, worn by Henry VIII at the Field of the Cloth of Gold and is now in the British Imperial State Crown.

Black Prince in formal dress

WOODSTOCK'S DEVELOPMENT

And how was the town changing over this time? Initially Woodstock grew quickly. By 1279, a hundred years after it was founded, there were 137 dwellings although apparently only 108 householders, suggesting that second homes were an issue even then. The total population is estimated as 540 inhabitants. This compares well with the fourteen adult men recorded in the Domesday Book for the five royal forests in this part of Oxfordshire although, when the park was first enclosed thirty years after the Domesday Book, one source claims *'very many farms'* were pulled down to permit Henry I's walling of the Park. Despite this early growth Woodstock's population in 1377 was only 255. The first outbreaks of plague – the Black Death – reached Oxfordshire in May 1359 and extracted a very heavy toll. Forty-two percent of the archdeaconry of Woodstock died. The term archdeaconry is curious since Woodstock was never more than a chapel of ease of Bladon but presumably the park and the demesne villages are intended here. This mortality rate was not unusual in those early plague years and Woodstock was lucky in that some Oxfordshire villages became non viable and disappeared from the map largely as a result of the plague. Even so, it was many years before the population of the town recovered. In 1469 there were estimated to be still only around 550 citizens living in 110 houses – much the same as in 1279.

From its earliest years New Woodstock had rights and privileges which enabled it to have its own local government since there is early documentation of this nature. These liberties existed by tradition only – a dangerous situation for troubled times. In 1453 the citizens of Woodstock appealed to King Henry VI for these rights to be recognised officially and Woodstock's Charter of Incorporation was given on May 24th 1453. The terms of this Charter were re-affirmed by Edward IV after Henry was deposed. Henry's Charter allowed the people of Woodstock and their successors to be free burgesses, to have a guild and a Guildhall together with a Mayor and Corporality. Woodstock was given a seal which was originally crowned with a knight's helmet but later, before the advent of the Marlboroughs, was topped with a ducal coronet. Freemen could elect a Mayor and a Sergeant at Mace. There would be a Portmoot court, that is an independent court with which county sheriffs, justices and Crown officers could not interfere. With these commitments came also possession of the whole borough so rents previously paid to the king came to the town. A pool, known as Le Pool, which the town rented from the king was given to the town for public use. Le Pool was probably the area now the town water meadows outside the Park. Meadows were extremely important to medieval farmers as they yielded hay which helped keep stock alive over the winter. In 1519 *'damage to the herbiage of the common pool ... by the horses of the King's servants'* incurred a fine of 13 shillings and fourpence.

In addition the Charter exempted the town from sending representatives to Parliament. No representation may have seemed an odd benefit but even then members' expenses were an issue. Someone had to pay for Members of Parliament (MPs) to go to London and to stay there. The exemption over representation ceased under Mary Tudor after which Woodstock sent two Members to Parliament until the Reform Act of 1832.

As London established itself as a leading city, the kings and the court spent more time there and moved around the country less. A series of comptrollers would supervise care of the King's Houses and the Park for the king or the queen and royal visits seem to have been less frequent. By the end of the Plantagenet era the King's Houses had developed into a rambling collection of buildings some of which were getting very old and perhaps in need of repair. The 'Palace' was beginning its long decline. For the Park and the town, the best years were still ahead.

3 The Tudors

ROBERT EDWARDS

HENRY VII

THE twenty-eight-year-old Henry Tudor came to power with the death of Richard III at the Battle of Bosworth Field in 1485. Henry's victory was achieved with the support of a coalition of families and factions determined to bring down Richard. As with many modern elections, victory owed more to general loss of support for the outgoing regime than to positive support for Henry's cause. Disillusion set in when Henry was seen to be ruling by threats of massive fines and confiscations. The rebellions led by Lambert Simnel and Perkin Warbeck were not the only threats to his tenure.

Henry Tudor had spent fourteen years in exile and detention at the courts of Brittany and France where he had witnessed the practice of *magnificence*. This was the system whereby the monarch set out to intimidate his subordinates against insurrection by a display of massive wealth. Potential opponents were made to feel powerless by the yawning gap between their own resources and those of the King.

As Henry VII, the King displayed his magnificence by accumulating silver plate and jewels and by a major building programme. The chapel of King's College at Cambridge had been started by his uncle Henry VI. He continued its construction and he intended that his palaces should also be seen to be worthy of a great monarch. One of the two estates where he began this process in 1494 was the Royal Manor of Woodstock. There he substantially rebuilt the buildings around the two existing courtyards and added a third court with a new fourteen roomed gatehouse. He probably built the (indoor) tennis court and channelled water from springs near the present High Lodge to supply the fountains and baths at the Manor. Part of this watercourse ran through a vaulted tunnel, the later rediscovery of which may have given rise to a variation on the mythical story of Fair Rosamund in which Queen Eleanor searches secret underground passages for Henry II's mistress.

Four thousand pounds were spent on Woodstock Manor over a nine year period – more than Henry spent on his brand new palace at Greenwich. Why Woodstock? Henry was a keen huntsman and falconer and the park with huge herds of deer must have been one attraction. The geographically central position in the kingdom and the distance from plague ridden towns could also have been significant.

Woodstock Manor House

In 1494 Henry VII was at Woodstock making arrangements for an elaborate ceremony at which his three-year-old second son Henry would be proclaimed Duke of York. This was a propaganda ploy to counteract the claim by a pretender to the throne, Perkin Warbeck, who said that *he* was Richard, Duke of York, the son of Edward IV and one of the two princes who had died in the Tower of London. The ceremony at Windsor would emphasise convincingly that Richard was dead and Henry made certain it would be well attended by combining it with the investiture of his three year old son as a Knight of the Bath. The attendance of a substantial number of other candidates for knighthood was guaranteed by the threat of massive fines for any absentees. Henry had developed the imposition of fines into a profitable industry.

In August 1497 Prince Arthur, heir to the throne and elder brother of the future Henry VIII, was formally betrothed to Princess Catherine of Aragon at Woodstock four years before his planned marriage. The Spanish ambassador stood in as proxy for the bride. This would have been an extravagant ceremony designed to impress the Spanish delegation with the importance of England. Henry VII would not have wanted to appear as the poor partner in this relationship so the choice of Woodstock for this event seems to indicate that this was no mere hunting lodge but one of the most spectacular residences in the land. Even so, building continued for a further six years during which time the Manor House reached the peak of its development.

Arthur died in 1502 a year after his marriage leaving the second son, also Henry, heir to the throne and freeing Catherine to become the first wife in this Henry's well-known saga of serial monogamy.

HENRY VIII

The overriding theme running through Henry VIII's reign was the need for a male heir. In June 1518, two years after the birth of her daughter Mary, Catherine of Aragon was at Woodstock and pregnant again. King Henry wrote to Cardinal Wolsey that he would not allow the Queen to be moved away from Woodstock *'at her dangerus tymes'* but these plans were abruptly changed in July when *'the sickness'* broke out among the court killing two men and infecting others. The royal family rapidly moved on to a healthier seat. Tragically Catherine gave birth to a stillborn daughter in October. Of her six children all were stillborn except Mary.

During another visit to Woodstock, in 1519, Henry intervened in a bitter dispute at Oxford University. The issue was whether the Bible should be studied in the original Greek or only in the official vulgate or medieval Latin version. Conservative churchmen considered the traditional interpretations and understandings of the Bible to be more important than the original text. The Word of God could only be understood through the intermediate pathway of the Church's teaching. Henry was advised by Sir Thomas More and other humanists who wanted to reform the Church from within. He took the side of those University scholars who studied the Bible in the original Greek by issuing a royal mandate to the University which commanded the study of the scriptures in their original languages.

Ten years later in 1529, shortly before he was appointed to replace Cardinal Wolsey as Lord Chancellor, Thomas More was again at Woodstock with the King and other members of the Council. The divorce from Catherine would have been the dominant business of the Council and More's opposition to this was already well known. Henry must have had enormous respect for More's ability for him to make his friend Lord Chancellor when they disagreed totally on the burning issue of the day.

After years of failure to persuade or even coerce Catherine to agree to a voluntary divorce or admission to a convent, Henry ostentatiously left her at Windsor in July 1531 and took Anne Boleyn with him to Woodstock. Was this the tipping point which finally persuaded Anne to become the King's mistress? It is accepted that she had been resisting his advances for several years in the hope of marriage. It is also certain (Elizabeth was born on 7th September 1533) that she was pregnant when Anne and Henry went through a nuptial ceremony in January 1533. This was before the divorce from Catherine. The rest is conjecture but what else was there for Anne to do at Woodstock?

In the first part of his reign Henry used Woodstock regularly but visits tailed off later because of his increasing immobility due to painful legs and massive obesity and because, by then, he had accumulated fifty residences from which to choose. This may explain why the Manor House was not in perfect condition when the young Elizabeth was sent there in 1554.

EDWARD VI

The main impact on Woodstock of young Edward VI's short reign was dissolution of the two chantry chapels whose resident priests had provided the borough with religious services. At least one of these clerics had been teaching in a chantry school built on the north side of the chancel of the church of St Mary Magdalene. The school is presumed to have closed. This was the impetus which drove Richard Cornwell, a Woodstock man who had prospered as a skinner (leather merchant) in London, to leave £300 in his will to found a grammar school in 1585. His school initially occupied the old chantry school room and continued to exist on various sites in the town until 1901. Cornwell's endowment fund survives as the Woodstock Exhibition Foundation which awards bursaries to apprentices and students

The Old Chantry School which became the Grammar School

from Woodstock families. Recent fundraising by the trustees and the generosity of several residents of the town has strengthened the reserves to the extent that Woodstock's oldest charity currently distributes up to four thousand pounds per year.

In 1549 Edward VI and his parliament passed an act that every church should use Thomas Cranmer's Protestant prayer book. All previous religious liturgy and written music for services had to be destroyed. Thousands of illuminated manuscripts were lost or the parchment (animal skin) on which they were written recycled by bookbinders. This explains the 1608 ledger in the Woodstock Borough archives called *A Booke of Chamberlins Accompts and the rents of the Borrghrough* (Borough) *of Newe Woodstocke* which has, as its outside cover, a well-worn sheet of mediaeval parchment on which writing and musical notation survive from a previous life.

From 1551 dates *An inquisition into the customs of Woodstock Manor.* "Customs" in this context meant the taxes to be paid by the seven surrounding villages and the feudal obligation on their inhabitants to cut and carry hay in the Park for the king's deer. The unfortunate inhabitants

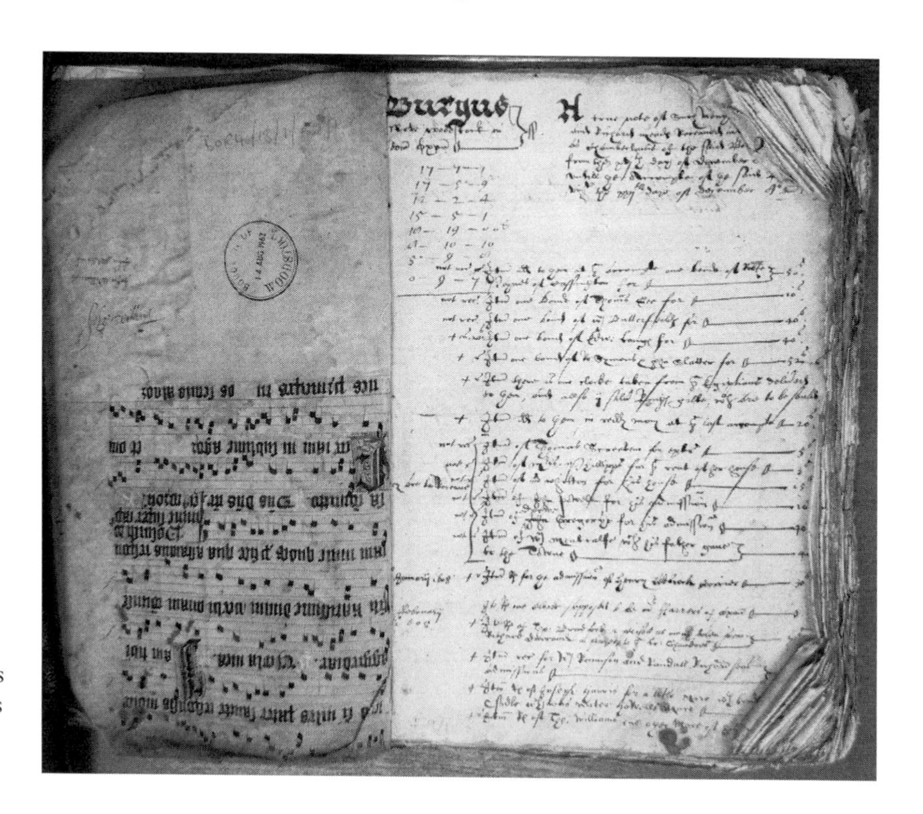

A Book of 'Chamberlins Accompts' and the rents of the Borough of New Woodstock

of Combe had to clean the Royal privies. This document states that *'All the mansion or manor place of the said demesnes, or bury lands for many years past have been decayed and prostrated'*. This has been misunderstood to mean that the Manor House was decayed. The entire document is about the villages of Hanborough, Combe, Stonesfield, Wootton, Old Woodstock, Hordley and Bladon which are frequently collectively referred to as the Manor of Woodstock so it is more likely that the decay refers to them and not to the royal residence.

ELIZABETH I

Princess Elizabeth at Woodstock. During the reign of her elder sister Mary, Elizabeth was sent, in May 1554, from the Tower of London to the Royal Manor House at Woodstock where she was detained until April 1555. She was guarded by one hundred soldiers and although she was allowed to walk in the gardens she could not receive visitors nor correspond with her friends and supporters. When she arrived the Manor House was reported to be in poor condition with no more than four rooms judged habitable and only three lockable doors. It is fair to suggest that this claim may have been exaggerated in order to extract royal funds for repairs. Sufficient repairs were eventually made so the soldiers, who initially camped in the open, could be indoors during the winter.

The background to Elizabeth's incarceration was one of religious strife, rebellion and fear of further insurrection. When Queen Mary came to the throne in 1553 she immediately replaced the compulsory Protestantism of her younger brother Edward VI with an equally mandatory return to Roman Catholicism. The Tudor dynasty had emerged precariously on the battle field of Bosworth from the highly unsettled period of the Wars of the Roses. Mary's three immediate predecessors had each faced serious rebellions against their rule. Her own accession had been challenged by the proclamation of Lady Jane Grey as Queen.

Sir Thomas Wyatt's revolt in Kent in 1554 was precipitated by the prospect of Mary's marriage to Philip of Spain. Wyatt was joined by the Navy and by many of the London trained bands who had been sent against him. With better planning and communications he could have linked up with reinforcements from Wales and the Midlands. He had anticipated support from committed Protestants, from those who feared that England would be dominated by the Pope in alliance with the Spanish superpower and from families who had profited from the destruction of the monasteries and feared that the Catholic Church might reclaim its possessions.

Clearly Wyatt would have put Elizabeth on the throne. Strenuous attempts, including the torture of Elizabeth's servants, were made to incriminate her in the rebellion but no proof was found. None the less both Stephen Gardiner, Bishop of Winchester and Lord Chancellor, and Renard, the equally influential Spanish Ambassador, counselled that Elizabeth would continue to be a figurehead for future rebellions and should be executed. The Princess justifiably feared a show trial or assassination. She would have been uncomfortably aware of the unpleasant precedent of the two Princes in the Tower and of Mary's huge grievance for the way Elizabeth's mother, Anne Boleyn, had humiliated both Mary and Mary's mother, Catherine of Aragon.

This was the context in which the twenty-year-old Elizabeth came to Woodstock in very real fear for her life. She was guarded there by Sir Henry

Bull Inn … later called the Angel Inn

Bedingfield, the Constable of the Tower of London. He limited her access to her household staff, several of whom were denied accommodation in the Manor and lodged at the Bull Inn. The Bull later became the Angel and in 1918 was replaced by the bank which is now the NatWest.

One of the people obliged to establish himself at the sign of the Bull was Thomas Parry, Elizabeth's cofferer, whose role was to oversee provisioning and payment of the Princess' household. Bedingfield expressed concern to the Privy Council at the endless comings and goings amongst Elizabeth's supporters and Parry's forty servants at the sign of the Bull. There were *'many more than have cause to repair there for a provision'*. In his biography of Elizabeth, Neale comments that the Bull was a *'barely disguised headquarters for Elizabeth's friends'* and *'Elizabeth and her servants were altogether too effervescent a company for the slow wit of her custodian'*. Youthful exuberance despite the risks of the times might explain the story that one of Elizabeth's gentlemen, wishing to make Elizabeth laugh, brought a goat before Sir Henry in the Manor House saying that the goat had been seen talking with Elizabeth in the garden, something for which Bedingfield's permission was needed, so he had brought the goat to Sir Henry for fear it was a Welshman in disguise.

Bedingfield's task was not just to keep Elizabeth out of mischief and political intrigue but to protect her from those, other than her sister, who might wish her harm. One night when Bedingfield was absent from the Manor House, a group of twenty-five *'disguised ruffians'* led by a man called Basset were surprised near Bladon Bridge trying to get into the Park so as to *'obtain access to the Lady Elizabeth on secret and important business'*, which business was assumed to be murder. Bedingfield seems to have sometimes used his own money to support the troops when the Privy Council were lax about paying them. Without this help would the guards have been less vigilant?

Excessively honest and unimaginatively dutiful though he was, Elizabeth's 'gaoler' referred to her as *'this great lady'*. Such respect probably helped Elizabeth negotiate with Bedingfield and she was eventually allowed to write to the Queen and to the Privy Council professing her total innocence and demanding to be charged and tried or set free to come to Court. Her letters were ignored. Paradoxically Elizabeth's chances of survival were increased by the marriage of Mary to Philip II of Spain in July 1554. Philip could see that if Elizabeth were removed from the succession the next in line would be the even less acceptable francophile Mary Queen of Scots, the widow of the Dauphin. If France could control both shores of the English Channel Philip's hold on the Netherlands would become precarious. After nearly a year's 'house arrest' at Woodstock, Elizabeth was released.

It is claimed that Elizabeth left two souvenirs behind in Woodstock. John Foxe's *Book of Martyrs* dated 1563 says that she had scratched '*with her diamond in a glass window very legibly*':

Much suspected of me
Nothing proved can be
Quoth Elizabeth, prisoner

Paul Hentzner, a German traveller, wrote in 1598 that he found the following lines written with coal (charcoal) on a shutter:

O Fortune! How thy restless wavering State
Hath fraught with Cares my troubled Wit!
Witness this present Prison whither Fate
Hath borne me, and the Joys I quit.
Thou causedst the Guilty to be loosed
From Bands, wherewith are Innocents inclosed:
Causing the Guiltless to be strait reserved,
And freeing those that Death had well deserved:
But by her Envy can be nothing wrought,
So God send to my foes all they have thought.
ELIZABETH Prisoner.
AD. MDLV (1555 Ed.)

Given the intelligence and prudence of Elizabeth it is highly unlikely that she would have put her name to these lines which could have been wilfully misinterpreted by lawyers looking for proof of treason. She would have taken utmost care to avoid the slightest hint of opposition to her sister. It is more probable that Hentzner witnessed the birth of Woodstock's tourist industry and that the site of the Queen's captivity was embellished for that purpose.

Elizabeth I and New Woodstock. Ballard claims that the inhabitants of the Borough treated Elizabeth with great courtesy during her captivity and that she later promised to give them a present '*In token of the happy change in my circumstances*'. In 1565 she granted to the Mayor and burgesses various properties which had belonged to the chantry of St Mary in return for an annual rent of four pounds. This was a commercial transaction which enabled the Crown to receive a lump sum rather than collect the rents separately. Partly because Elizabeth managed her estates so carefully, she

2–8 Park Street today

amassed a reserve of one million pounds by the time of the Armada (1588) enabling her to pay for that famous defence.

In 1974 Woodstock Borough was amalgamated into the new West Oxfordshire District Council. The successor Town Council which now had the same status as a parish council claimed that numbers 2–8 Park Street, which included the Post Office, had been part of Queen Elizabeth's 'gift'. Indeed the Borough had still been paying £4-6s-8d as chantry rent although this was now paid to the Dukes of Marlborough. An arbitrator accepted this claim and awarded ownership of these buildings to the new Town Council, not to the District Council, on the grounds that the buildings were part of the ancient heritage of the town.

1575: *The Woodstock Entertainment*. Following her coronation Elizabeth I and her court stayed at Woodstock on four occasions in spite of the unhappy memories the Manor must have held for her. The Royal Manor and the Park were being managed by Sir Henry Lee who has been variously described as the Steward, Ranger, Master of the Game, Parker and Lieutenant of the Park. He held office for thirty years. He had the use of a residence called High Lodge which was not on the site of the present building near Combe Gate but was situated close to the Royal Manor.

Lee had first come to the notice of the Queen through his outstanding skill at jousting and was appointed as her champion with responsibility for creating the magnificent pageantry of her annual Accession Day tournaments at Whitehall. There the knights appeared in ostentatious costumes to heap praises on Elizabeth in elaborate allegories before showing their skill in the tiltyard. For Elizabeth I's five-week visit to Woodstock Manor in 1575 Henry Lee wrote and presented a complex outdoor entertainment which she watched at first from *'a fine bower made of purpose covered with greene iuie* [ivy] *and seates made of earthe with sweet-smelling hearbes'*. Two mythical knights fought for the hand of Caudina but were stopped by Hermetes the hermit who urged her to choose for herself. The story went on and on with increasing complexity for two days with the Fayry Queen arriving to advise and direct. A short synopsis by Matthew Woodcock runs to a thousand words. Lee was well aware that too much mythology on an empty stomach could be indigestible so substantial banquets interrupted the proceedings. At the climax of the tale a noble knight chooses to serve *'the common weales good plight'* instead of proposing to his fair lady. In other words he chooses to work for the good of all instead of following his emotional preference for the lady. This was Lee's thinly veiled counter attack against the Earl of Leicester's recent extravagant entertainment at Kenilworth Castle which had set out to show the Earl as a worthy suitor for the royal hand. Lee and his advisers, who would have included Lord Burleigh, were more in favour of a match with the French Duke of Alençon in order to cement an alliance with France against Spain.

Henry Lee has here invented the character of the Fairy Queen who subsequently re-emerged as a feature of the Accession Day tournament mythology and was then adopted by Edmund Spenser for his glorification of Queen Elizabeth I called *The Faerie Queene* which, although massively unfinished, is by far the longest poem in the English language.

The Stuarts, the Civil War and After

4

CHRISTOPER COOPER · HANNAH COOPER
POPPY LAMBERT · JOHN BANBURY

JAMES I

JAMES I first stayed in the Manor House at Woodstock shortly after his accession in 1603 and it rapidly became a favoured country residence of this austere monarch. The house was in some disrepair following years of disuse. The court, suited to the extravagance and magnificence of English Tudor monarchs, felt it unfit for royal habitation. Sir Robert Cecil, with the King on that first visit, found it an '*unwholesome*' and '*uneaseful*' place with the house standing on springs (of water) and '*no savours except cows and pigs*'. Most of the royal household had to be lodged in tents. Scottish James' view of what was fit for royal habitation differed greatly from that of the court.

The King and Queen developed lasting relationships with the local community both within Woodstock and further afield during several significant visits between 1605 and 1624. For example, in August 1605, just before the Gunpowder Plot, the royal couple spent three days hunting at Woodstock and killed two stags which James gave to the Chancellor and Vice Chancellor of Oxford University. James and his queen, Anne, often sought a hearty meal and good company at Ditchley Park Hall, home of Sir Henry Lee, five miles outside Woodstock. There a stag James caught in 1608 is mounted on the wall with a plaque describing the final moments of its life. James' friendship with the Lees was marked by James knighting Henry Lee in September 1614 and making George Lee Baron of Whaddon at a lavish ceremony in August 1616.

In 1610 the King, the Queen and James' eldest son Henry, Prince of Wales, enjoyed a two-day stay with stags bagged at Ditchley and Cornbury.

Another visit in August 1612 witnessed six days of feasting and entertainment. However 1612 was plunged into grief when Prince Henry died of typhoid fever. The diagnosis seems likely although some report Henry died after a game of 'real tennis', not at Woodstock, when he had not fully recovered from a bout of pneumonia. Despite James' grief, it was five years before he paid Henry's debts of £13 6s 6d to a Woodstock shoe maker, Thomas Wilson, although at the same time he did pay for an apprentice to be trained by Wilson. Henry's sudden death made the unfortunate second son Prince Charles heir apparent and shortly thereafter Prince of Wales.

James' relations with the local community were not all cordial. In 1617 the forest of Wychwood had its limits extended and thus Forest Law extended, leading local communities to petition Parliament to redress this grievance. A humble petition from the inhabitants of Wotton, Hordley, Oulde Woodstock, Bladon, Stonesfield, Coombe and Handborough complained of the denial of their rights and livelihood.

CHARLES I

In 1625 James died and his son Charles became King of England. He paid a visit to the Manor House in 1625 where the court met in August of that year. He was fleeing the *'prevailing sickness'* which had gripped the capital and he clearly saw his country estate as a salubrious alternative. A soldier from Norwich visiting a few years later in 1633 described the Manor House as a palace within a great court protected by a substantial gatehouse. A significant flight of steps led up to an aisled hall hung with tapestries. Off the hall was a chapel where the observer described a curious font, many curious windows and a roof *'most admirably wrought'*. Was this a decorative plaster ceiling? From there he went into a number of presence, privy and bed chambers with views over the walled garden or to the town beyond the tennis court. He goes on to describe the area where he understood Elizabeth had been imprisoned and indicates there were many other rooms. Finally from the roof of the gatehouse he looked over the Park and the nearby chief ranger's house, High Lodge, which seems to have been somewhere to the west of the Manor House. His comments on the ruins of Rosamund's bower were mentioned earlier (p. 19) but Crossley states that there were still twenty foot high walls and pillars at the Bower until the beginning of the Civil War when they were flattened to avoid attacking troops using them as cover.

THE CIVIL WAR

Charles' determination to raise money through taxation which had not been approved by Parliament was a major contribution to his downfall. Oxfordshire was first assessed for Ship Tax in 1635 and was one of the first inland counties obliged to pay the Tax. Woodstock was largely royalist and paid its first annual instalment of £20 2s 2d without recorded complaint. Only thirty citizens were deemed eligible for taxation and half the instalment was paid by only eight citizens. The next year the contribution was estimated at

Ship Money writ from Charles I, written in Latin in 17th-century Chancery script states: 'Charles by the Grace of God …'

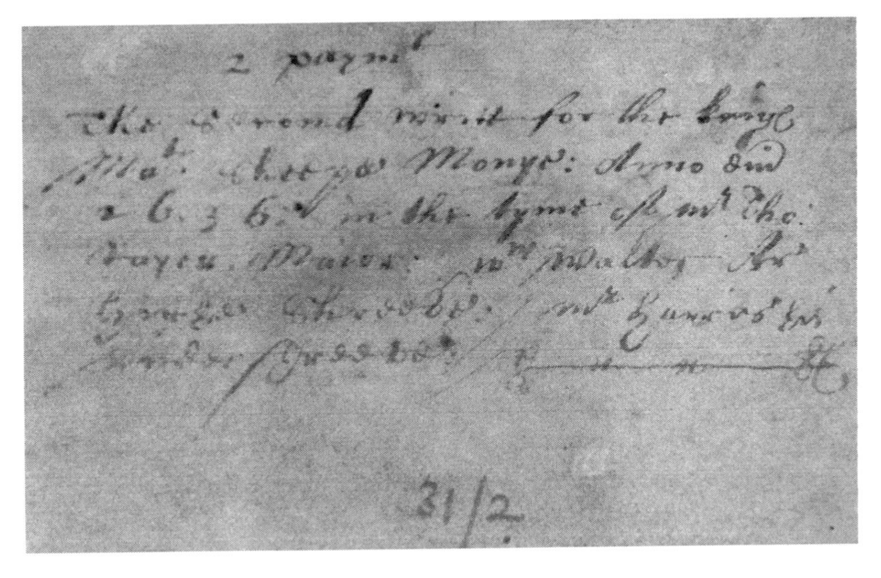

Payment record for Ship Tax: '2nd payment. The second writ for the King's Majesty's ship money anno domini 1636 in the time of Mr Thomas Rayer Mayor'

Plaque to Edmond Hiorne – Park Street

fifteen pounds. By contrast, Banbury and Chipping Norton, both of which were taxed at thirty pounds, paid very reluctantly and, in Banbury, only after the town constables had been gaoled. Overall Oxfordshire proved one of the most difficult counties in which to collect the Tax. In neighbouring Buckinghamshire John Hampden, father-in-law of Woodstock's MP William Lenthall, was encouraging the people to refuse to pay and, up the Banbury road at Broughton Castle, William Fiennes Lord Saye and Sele was persistent in his opposition to the Tax.

Once war broke out, Woodstock's vital position on the route to the King's headquarters at Oxford and its role as a stronghold of the royalist movement made it an object of Parliamentarian desire and one of the more significant places in the area during the Civil War. Being on a North-South road into Oxford and the Thames crossing meant both Royalists and Parliamentarians had vested interests in Woodstock so it was almost inevitable that it would witness considerable action in the Civil War. This created problems. Early in the War, armies seemed to march through Woodstock with little interest in the Manor House. Communication between Manor House and the King in Oxford was relatively unencumbered. In 1642 Royalist forces were quartered in the town and were given the town armoury by the Town Clerk Edmund Hiorne who also posted a proclamation against the Parliamentarian Earl of Essex. Shortly afterwards Parliamentarian troops passed through Woodstock and sacked Hiorne for having given away the armoury. They forced him to apologise in the House of Commons on his knees in front of the Speaker. Hiorne was reinstated at the Restoration but died shortly afterwards. His history is described briefly on a blue plaque on the wall of a house just west of the church in Park Street which states *'Edmund Hiorne ... Appointed Town Clerk 1607. For his courageous loyalty to King Charles was dismissed with ignominy by Parliament but reinstated at the restoration of the monarchy. Died 1665'*. The Speaker was Woodstock's MP. Despite being predominantly royalist, Woodstock had returned William Lenthall, a keen defender of the rights of Parliament, as MP. He was a wealthy lawyer who was Recorder for Woodstock and Master of the Rolls as well as Speaker. Elected Speaker at the beginning of the 1640 Long Parliament, he was one of the most influential men in Britain and in effect the voice of Parliament. His statement – when Charles invaded the Commons, took the Speaker's chair

William Lenthall MP for Woodstock, Speaker of the House of Commons 1640

and tried to arrest five MPs who opposed his policies – is often quoted in relation to the Speaker's position: *'May it please your Majesty, I have neither eyes to see nor tongue to speak in this place but as the House is pleased to direct me, whose servant I am here.'*

In July 1642 the King was staying at Woodstock with Prince Rupert, the Duke of York and most of his army to escape the plague in Oxford. The old Manor House was defended to the extent that it was considered a castle. Its defences may have been designed by the famous Dutch military architect, Bernard de Gomme, who designed those at Oxford which were far superior to anything the Parliamentarians had created at that point. Earthworks were still identifiable in Blenheim Park some 200 years later. Woodstock became one of a chain of strong points which encircled Oxford with the purpose of deterring the enemy from advancing too close to the city.

The King's humbling at Edgehill near Banbury on 23rd October 1642 resulted in expansion of the Woodstock garrison by two hundred Banbury men from the Lord Lieutenant General's Regiment of Musketeers. These were the most skilled and the most expensive troops in the King's army.

Location of the Battles fought in the Civil War with insert of the Manor House under siege

They would have camped in the Manor grounds, with their commanders put up either in the luxurious state rooms of the gatehouse or in the pubs and inns of Woodstock. Whilst in Woodstock they were mainly engaged in training (and in drinking). They were training both soldiers and enthusiastic local volunteers, who were divided into squadrons. *'After they had beyn reasonably instructed in the words of Commaund and in their postures, they were put into battell arraye and skirmished together in a very decent manner'.* Training consisted of mock battles and was greatly superior to that of the Roundheads at this point in the war although surpassed later by that of Cromwell's New Model Army. The Banbury Musketeers soon moved on to counter threats from Parliamentary forces in other parts of England.

The First Battle of Newbury in 1643, a pivotal moment in the Civil War, claimed the life of the Earl of Carnarvon, the Steward of Woodstock. This must have dented the morale of the Royalist garrison as he was a respected figurehead for local supporters of the King. The role of the Steward of Woodstock was, along with the Mayor and Aldermen, one of the most important positions in Woodstock. He was the king's representative in Woodstock, and oversaw the running of Manor House and Park.

Then, in 1644, General Waller and his Parliamentarian forces unexpectedly invaded the county. The King was dining at Woodstock after killing a brace of bucks hunting in the Park. He heard Waller was at Eynsham and he withdrew in haste that night to Oxford. On July 17th Waller's forces arrived at the Manor House and the captain came out of the House to parley – and was arrested. The house surrendered without loss of life. Waller demanded that the keepers of the King's Parks give two large bucks to his soldiers. The request was refused with the resulting threat of *'contempt of* [Waller's] *wrath'* and if they *'faile to send the Bucks,* [Waller] *shall not faile to fetch you if you dare to lye in your houses'.* It does not seem to be reported whether Waller got his way or not.

However the Parliamentarians did not occupy the Manor House for long. By September the Manor House was back in Royalist hands. After that the King sent the body of his forces to Woodstock to withstand the anticipated Parliamentarian threat. This must have brought a huge number of people to the small town as it would not have been just the army, but those who follow and serve an army as well: blacksmiths, surgeons and doctors, soldiers and supporters' wives, servants for the King and peasants picked up in surrounding villages and armed with primitive weapons.

This vast army of people would have put great strain on Woodstock and the surrounding areas. Not only did the occupation affect the town but great shortages developing in Oxford affected the whole county. To deal with the ever-increasing deprivations, the '*King hath commanded the constables inhabiting within the seventeen parishes next adjoining Oxford to bring in straw, hay, oates and all other provisions whatsoever to bee imployed for his majesties service*'. Woodstock was one of these seventeen parishes and, for a town already stretched beyond its means, such extra pressures were particularly unwelcome. Shortages in Oxfordshire were so severe that one of the King's agents was reported to have paid two shillings a night for his horses' hay. To give some idea of the inflated prices, a shilling was almost a week's pay for an average worker. Hay was probably unaffordable for agricultural workers and livestock prices plummeted.

The Civil War was the first occasion for which the whole country was geared towards war, something not seen again until the Great War of 1914–18 and then the fighting was overseas. Civilians, as well as soldiers, experienced their fair share of hardship not only at the hands of hostile forces. The people of Woodstock were subjected to the demands of an occupying Royalist army and, although not politically hostile, the occupying forces would have pilfered local supplies with little regard to ownership. The Great Fire of Oxford only made the situation worse. On Sunday 8th October 1644 a fire, started by soldiers roasting a coveted pig, spread as a high wind blew the flames southward leaving a path of devastation and destruction in its wake. Pressure for accommodation on neighbouring towns and villages such as Woodstock increased. High taxes, disruption by warfare as well as the damage caused by the fire wearied the local people exposed to so many hardships.

That autumn the Royalist Garrison of Winchester surrendered to the Parliamentarian forces, and as a result of their surrender retreated to Woodstock. Woodstock was again a staging post for the Royalist army and one can only imagine the total despair the local populace now felt from the prolonged chaos. '*Seven hundred foote and one hundred horse*', a vast number of men, led by the Earl of Northumberland, assembled in Woodstock before marching to counter the Parliamentarian forces present at Banbury. Despite the Royalist troops, further Parliamentarian raids on the town resulted in the loss of fifty royalist horses and a great many prisoners although an unprovoked Parliamentarian raid in February 1646 on the garrison at Woodstock was repulsed. The attackers fled in the face of fierce gunfire from the defending citizens.

The defence of the Manor House and town was now entrusted to Captain Samuel Fawcett, who refortified the building with artificial

Image of Stuart coin

earthworks where natural features were insufficient. During the work, the Palace was vulnerable so Fawcett broke cover and attacked the Parliamentarian raiders who had seized the opportunity to besiege the weakened Royalist stronghold. Despite all this defence, Parliamentarian Colonel George Fleetwood, brother to the Ranger of Woodstock Sir William Fleetwood, managed to sever all communications between Woodstock and the King's headquarters at Oxford. The Parliamentarians believed if Woodstock was isolated it would fall swiftly and with minimal effort on their part. Their first attack on the Manor failed miserably. The defences withstood the onslaught and for the death of just five Royalists, one hundred Parliamentarians were killed. Colonel Rainsborough then tried to batter the Royalist Garrison into submission with a lengthy artillery barrage. The Manor House was partially destroyed and the besieged garrison had to shelter in the remains of earthworks and fortifications. After twenty days the siege ended when Sir William Fleetwood, the Earl of Southampton and the Earls of Ashburnham and Lindsey were sent from Oxford to instruct the Manor House to surrender with the town to Colonel Rainsborough on agreed terms. Fawcett and his men were granted safe passage to Oxford with battle honours completely intact and standards flying high. The next day the King left Oxford.

The English Civil War ended but the devastation that had engulfed Britain since the war began did not. The Manor House at Woodstock was severely damaged and considered indefensible although parts do seem to have been suitable for habitation for many years afterwards. Materials and treasures were removed and sequestered by local people. Wood and stone were taken in bulk to repair houses; furniture and interior panelling were secreted away by savvy local businessmen and thieves for resale later. What was left following the bombardment and lootings was listed by Cromwell's commissioners and sold on to cover war expenses. However the commissioners had problems. 'Disturbances' at the Manor House, whilst it was being surveyed, were such that the commissioners abandoned the House and their survey, retiring to Ewelme to complete their report.

The disturbances at the Manor House. These disturbances are romanticised in Walter Scott's novel *Woodstock* but John Aubrey in *Miscellanies upon Various Subjects* includes a letter, received from John Lyall of Trinity College Oxford, which reports a tale told by a Mr Hawes who lived with Sir William Fleetwood in the Park. '*The four surveyors which were sent to measure the park, and lodged themselves with some other companions in the manor, were pelted out of their chambers by stones thrown in at the windows; but from what* *hands the stones came they could not see; that their candles were continually put out, as fast as they lighted them; and that one with his sword drawn to defend a candle, was with his own scabbard in the mean time well cudgelled'*. They fled '*some of them to Sir William Fleetwood's house, and the rest to some other places'*. Plot in his *Natural History of Oxford-shire* gives vivid descriptions of a poltergeist who *came into the bedchamber in the shape of a dog which going under the bed did as it were gnaw the bedchord'*. Another creature '*came into the withdrawing room treading much like a bear'*. Other descriptions were of grievous noises, stinking ditchwater and three dozen trenchers thrown out of a bedchamber window. Plot is clearly doubtful whether they really were supernatural events but explains the disturbances were attributed to the Just Devil of Woodstock. This Just Devil turned out to be a royalist named Joe Collins who had managed to get himself employed by Cromwell's men. He was never apprehended nor punished.

THE AFTERMATH OF THE CIVIL WAR

The economic effect of the War on the people of Woodstock would have been profound. Woodstock's three main industries – bell founding, glove making and inn keeping – remained strong but the war did have an impact.

Part of the Charles II Charter of the Borough of Woodstock 1664

The connection with royalty and the court and the employment that went with activities at the Manor House had gone. The majority of the town's young men would have been drafted into various armies and the young healthy male population much depleted. Under Cromwell's puritanical regime the demand for church bells decreased as the churches became simpler and poorer. Demand for gloves dropped as the exquisite needlework of Woodstock gloves was frowned upon as frivolous and anyway few families could afford such frivolities after the looting of royalist estates. Inn keeping was also affected as alcohol was actively discouraged and in some places banned but the demand for hospitality for the many travellers to Oxford would have remained as the city remained a centre of education and commerce.

THE LATTER PART OF THE SEVENTEENTH CENTURY

In 1649 the Manor House and estate was leased to Lt. Col Fleetwood, Col Cooke, and Col Buttler by the Parliamentary Surveyors for £300 per annum to be paid to Mr Walter Whetton, who appears to have been responsible for collecting the levy. The survey of the house recorded the remaining walls and courtyard of the old Manor House in acres, roods and perches. The total site was over three acres and some ideas of the House's appearance can be gained from a number of engravings made between 1690 and 1730. How accurately the engravers showed the House may have depended on their imagination as much as their knowledge.

The Civil War had changed the lives of those who lived in or around Woodstock Park but with the death of Cromwell in 1658 and, in 1660, a *'free Parliament and the restoration of government by Kings, Lords and Commons'*, trade improved. Glovers and dealers in skins could once again benefit from hunting in the Park and the return of visitors to the town.

One of the first actions of the restored Charles II was to recover lands and properties sold during the Commonwealth period. At Woodstock this also meant stopping the wholesale felling and disposal of those trees left in the Park and stopping the cutting and removal of hay and other products from the estate as well as cancelling whatever permits and leases had been agreed since May 1642. In all this Charles was helped by Sir William Fleetwood who was appointed Warden of the Park and estates around 1662. Purchase of 60 acres of land known as Combe Lays to enlarge the Park caused controversy in Combe with former tenants of the land arguing that some common land had also been taken. They lost common

By the Lords Justices

Tho. Cantuar:
J Somers C.S.
Pembroke C.P.S.
Devonshire
Shrewsbury
Dorset

Wee do hereby direct & require you that you fairly kill & deliver to the Bearer hereof a Brace of fatt Bucks of this Season for the use of the Vice Chancellor of Oxford And for so doing this shall be your Warrant Att the Court at Whitehall the 19th day of June 1696 in the eighth yeare of his Maties Reigne

To the Keeper or Underkeepers of Woodstock Park

Privy Council's demand note to deliver a 'brace of fatt bucks' in 1696

rights and also lost profits they might have made from using these rights … especially as it took them over three years to get compensation.

Keepers of the Manor changed frequently. In 1665 Montague Bertie, who had been a distinguished commander and had been wounded in the Civil War, was appointed. When he died after only five months he was succeeded by the Earl of Clarendon, who was to be lieutenant and governor of Woodstock, with the annual sum of £80: £40 for wages and £40 for hay for the deer in the Park. His tenure came to an end in 1667 when he was impeached and went into exile.

In 1658 John Wilmot, born at Ditchley and a favourite of Charles II, succeeded to the title of Earl of Rochester. His father who had joined Charles in his escape after the battle of Worcester, was created Earl of Rochester and continued to have a successful military career. While performing his duties as custodian of the Park, John Wilmot lived in High

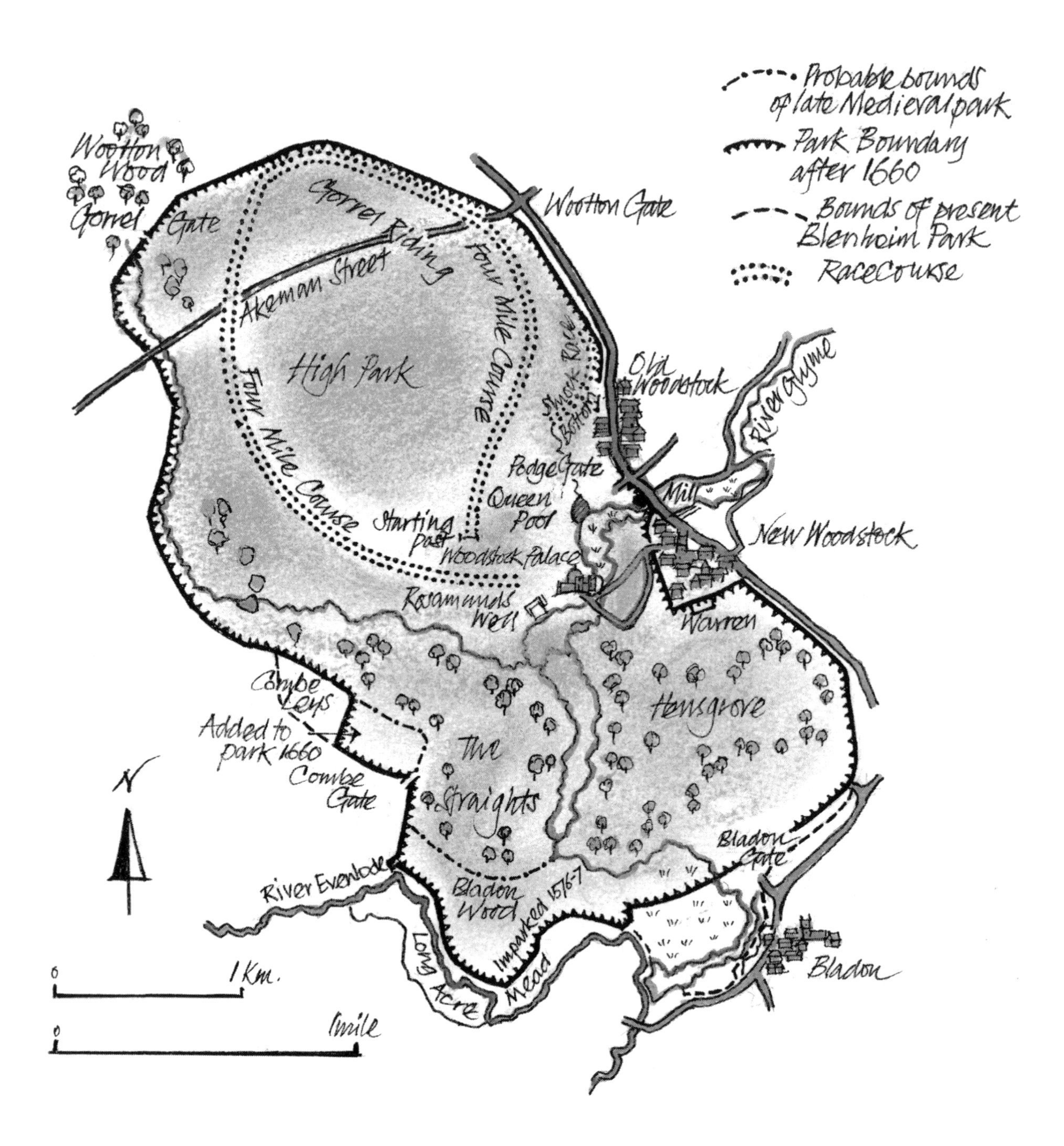

Map 4 The Royal Park – 17th century Showing the Racecourse and the realigned Southern Boundary

Lodge, still the wooden structure which had been the home of Sir Henry Lee in Queen Elizabeth's reign. High Lodge remains today although rebuilt in stone on several occasions and no longer in its original position.

The King and the Duke of York visited Woodstock Park in late summer of 1663, when the Court was at Oxford and in 1664 Woodstock was granted a new charter. Parliament never voted Charles II enough money to run the country so he insisted that hundreds of towns needed new charters. He then provided these charters in exchange for substantial fees. The Mayor and some of the Aldermen and Councillors who had been ousted by commissioners in 1662 because of Parliamentary leanings were re-appointed although the Crown reserved the right to approve the appointment of Steward, Recorder and Town Clerk.

Another visitor in 1664, John Evelyn, commented on the destruction caused to the old royal seat and park by the rebel army when he passed through on his way from Oxford to Cornbury. Destroyed or not, John Lord Lovelace took over the old gatehouse, the only habitable part remaining of the old Manor House, around 1670. He instigated horse racing in the Park with races run, in 1688 at least, for a £50 prize plate. Later race meetings included stag hunts, coursing, foot races and women's smock races. The race course was about four miles in length running from just north of the old Manor House, north-west towards Ditchley Gate and returning in a sweeping circle to finish back at the Manor. The running track for the other races was closer to the eastern wall of the Park. Horse-racing continued until 1722 with the Duke's landscape design allowing the course space between newly planted trees.

Another 17th century journal writer, Celia Fiennes, whose descendants still hold Broughton Castle near Banbury, passed through Woodstock on one of her famous journeys on this occasion from London to Herefordshire. She comments on Woodstock Manor House *'where remaines no foote steps of faire Rosomonds Bower, only ye walls round ye parke and the little brookes that supply'd it with water for ye baths and wells and ponds'*

For many years kings had made only brief and sporadic visits to Woodstock. Hunting had lost its popularity and horse and foot races did not attract the crowds that the King's Court had brought. The park still produced the king's deer and a document from 1696 shows killing deer was regulated such that *'a brace of fatt bucks of the season'* was subject to a properly issued order from the Archbishop of Canterbury and the Privy Council before being delivered to the Vice Chancellor of Oxford University for his feasting. Woodstock Park was ready for change.

5 The Coming of the Churchills

JOHN BANBURY · MONICA HOLMES-SIEDLE
ELIZABETH POSKITT

PREVIOUS chapters have referred to the gradual decline of Woodstock Manor House as a royal residence. The Civil War had left little of value in the villages. The Manor House had been ransacked but not totally destroyed. Letters written in the late 16th and in the 17th centuries describe a crumbling Manor House with dilapidated walls surrounded by neglected woodlands and overall *'dereliction of the Manor'* (implying the surrounding villages as well as the Park). Engravings made some years after the end of the Civil War show that the Manor House still had walls and a substantial gatehouse but it was reported as uninhabitable, in a filthy condition and used as a stable for cows and horses.

Since the reign of Edward II it had been the custom for the Manor to be given as a dowry to queens who gained income from the tenants and villages. Use by the sovereign had diminished greatly over the years. James II visited in 1687 during a royal progress around the country and was said, by Macaulay who was writing over a century later, to have dined *'in great state at the palace of Woodstock'*. This occasion was probably the last royal entertainment of any significance at the Manor House.

Was it Queen Anne's own idea or was the idea suggested to her when, late in 1704, she mooted the gift of Woodstock Manor to John Churchill, Duke of Marlborough as reward for his successes against the French in the Wars of the Spanish Succession? Green suggests that Anne developed the idea of the gift in discussion with Churchill's wife, Anne's great friend and devoted servant, Sarah Jenyns (Jennings is the spelling more widely used). Sarah seemed to take to the idea rather more readily than Anne had expected possibly because Sarah was finding life at court rather tedious. Her husband was even more enthusiastic.

SARAH JENNINGS AND JOHN CHURCHILL

Sarah was from a prosperous Somerset family of landed gentry living in St Albans at the time of her birth. Sarah, ten years younger than John Churchill, was born on June 1st 1660 although she liked to say that she had been born on May 29th, the date of Charles II's accession. She grew up in Holywell House but after the death of her father the family moved to apartments at St James' Palace. From here thirteen-year-old Sarah joined the Duke of York's household to care for Anne, the Duke's second daughter by his first wife. John Churchill was also in the Duke's household at that time and it is there that the couple met.

When he first met Sarah in the early 1670s, John Churchill was in a group of wild young aristocrats known as 'The Wits'. For three years he had maintained a liaison with his cousin Barbara Villiers, Duchess of Cleveland and one of Charles II's mistresses. She is reputed to have given Churchill £4,500 which he invested in a life annuity giving an annual income of £500, in return for keeping their liaison secret. There was no secret. The Duchess gave birth to a third daughter in 1672 named Barbara whom even the King, whilst providing for the child, had no doubt was John Churchill's child not his own. Hibbert says a contemporary court rumour suggested that when Churchill decided to marry Sarah, he broke off his liaison with Barbara by encouraging a young nobleman to have a bath in his rooms and then lie naked on a couch turned away from the door. Barbara, described once by a bishop as '*ravenous*', came into the room, mistook the young man … at which point: enter John Churchill.

The suggestion of marriage between Sarah and John was opposed by John's father who needed John to marry a rich heiress but marry they did although the time and date of the wedding remain a mystery. In those early years of marriage Sarah was away from court keeping house. John Churchill had recently refused a legacy from his grandfather in favour of his father and was not well off so early married life was relatively impoverished. This experience honed Sarah's well-known skill of paring budgets to the minimum, something which stayed with her all her life.

In 1683 Princess Anne married and invited Sarah back to join her household as Lady of the Stole. Churchill was busy abroad on diplomatic missions or leading armies in skirmishes although he was also one of the Lords of the Bedchamber to King Charles II. When James II came to the throne, John Churchill was at the forefront of the troops that put down the Monmouth rebellion but James proved an unpopular and controversial sovereign. Although purporting loyalty when sent to confront William of Orange's invading troops in south-west England, Churchill and many others went over to William's side, thus effecting the Great and Glorious Revolution of 1688/9. Sarah, for whom James had issued an arrest warrant in view of her husband's treachery, fled with Princess Anne (who was ready to jump out of the window rather than face her father) to Nottingham until James fled into exile. Shortly after these events Churchill was made the Earl of Marlborough.

THE GIFT OF THE MANOR OF WOODSTOCK

Time passed. Marlborough amassed victories and honours. Anne conferred a Dukedom on him after her accession in 1702 but Marlborough's victory leading the Allied Armies with Prince Eugene at the Battle of Blindheim in Bavaria in the summer of 1704 seemed to demand an even more extraordinary honour. Parliament made addresses of gratitude for Marlborough's victories but could not decide how to perpetuate his triumph. They accepted Anne's suggestion of Woodstock Manor with alacrity. With a large gift of Treasury money to put the estate in order Woodstock Park could be restored and maintained and would no longer be a royal responsibility. In addition Anne knew her confidante and lady-in-waiting Sarah Churchill would be only one day's ride from court. Thus, early in 1705 Parliament agreed the gift of *'the Honour and Manor of Woodstock'* together with Woodstock Park, itself alone nearly 2000 acres, and the demesne villages. With this gift of the estate and unspecified public funds for a new building, the Churchills came to Woodstock Park.

The Park was crown land but the only 'quit-rent' demanded for this estate was, and still is, a standard bearing three gilded fleur-de-lys on a field argent, copying the standard of Louis XIV's *Corps du Roi*. The most recent standard is hung annually above the bust of Marlborough in the Guard Room at Windsor. It is presented on August 2nd, the date of the battle using the old Julian calendar rather than August 13th, the date in the modern calendar.

Once the gift was decided, Queen Anne's surveyor Christopher Wren visited the Park and came back with the view that the work would cost the Treasury £100,000. Sarah was horrified at the expense but in the end the Treasury paid nearly two and a half times as much as this and the Marlboroughs still had to finish the Palace with their own money. The Duke also visited Woodstock with his architect John Vanbrugh for

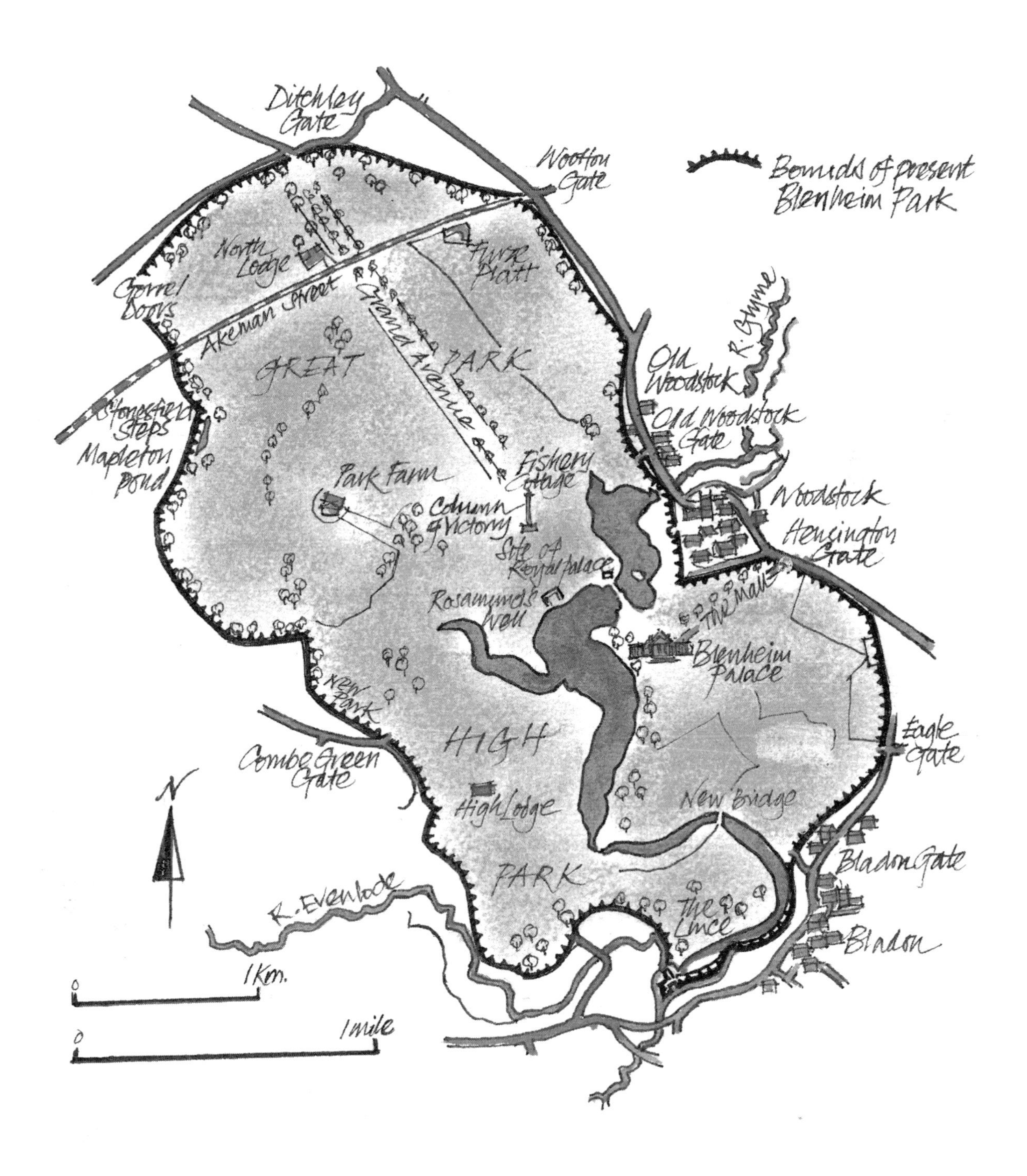

Map 5 Blenheim Park 18th to 21st century Remodelled by Lancelot (Capability) Brown

preliminary decisions about what was going to be a substantial building. Despite being involved in the original inspection, Wren was not chosen as the architect. Instead John Vanbrugh was chosen, perhaps because he and the Duke were both members of the Whig toasting (ie drinking toasts) Kit Cat club. From the beginning Sarah was against this appointment and from the following years come tales of endless wrangling and dispute between architect and Duchess.

Blenheim Castle, as it was originally called, would occupy a raised area south of the River Glyme allowing fine views in all directions. A view south over flat open woodland could be cleared and opened to a vista several miles long which would be contained in width by planting new groups of trees. Old oaks from the hunting forest could be conserved to show the heritage of the site. To the north there would be a grand entrance court with a long ceremonial drive to the old north gate past the ruined Manor House on the farther bank of the Glyme. The view west was across the river to the trees of the ancient forest. The Duke agreed the programme of works with Vanbrugh, who had engaged Nicholas Hawksmoor as assistant, and then returned to the Continent to pursue the war leaving Sarah at court with the Queen.

This building would be in the grandiose French style used by the Sun King, Louis XIV. The original plans for the Park left the old Manor House on its bluff as a romantic ruin mouldering in time whilst a grand bridge almost as long and as high as the palace itself spanned the river. This bridge presented problems. Those commenting mention the steep slopes and even crags down to the river. This aspect of the landscape is less obvious today after the valley has been filled by the lake and after the dramatic earth shifting of Capability Brown. In addition to these basic decisions there were plans for extensive landscape works, flower gardens, parterre, a walled kitchen garden and the planting of several thousand trees, some young and small and some more mature so the Park design could appear more quickly.

THE BUILDING OF BLENHEIM

Not everyone was happy with the concept of the new Castle at Woodstock. There are suggestions that the Queen's tenants in the Park were far from pleased at being moved out. Some seem to have been slow to go but eventually they did all leave and at 6pm on June 18 1705 the foundation stone of the Castle was laid amid great festivities. There was

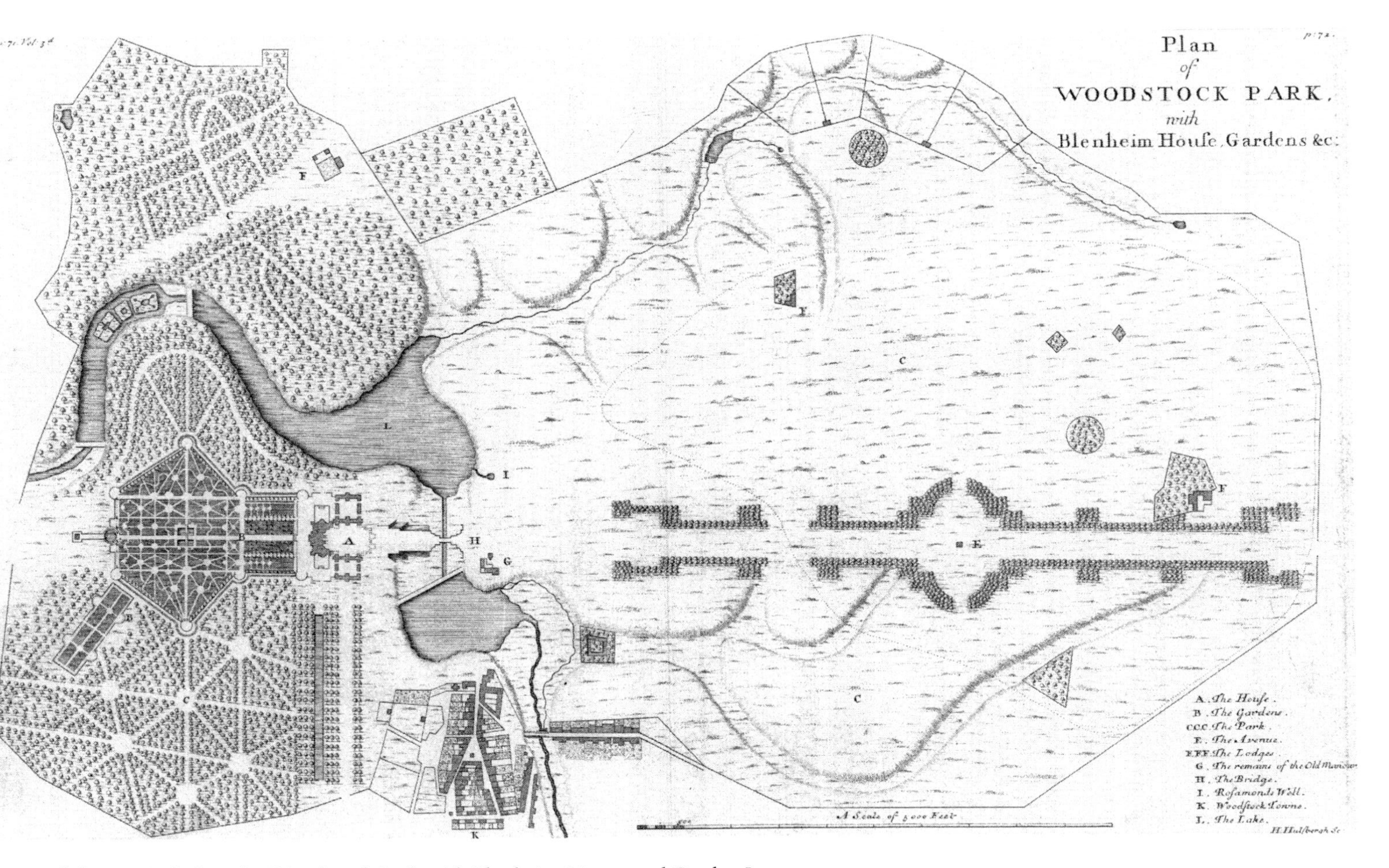

One of the original plans for Woodstock Park with Blenheim House and Garden Layouts

dancing from three different sets of Morris dancers: young men, young women and *'old beldames'*. There was no shortage of alcohol and afterwards the company went to Woodstock Town Hall where the gentry were treated to more drinks and cakes whilst the common people were given ale and cakes at the Town Cross.

From the beginning there were problems. Five quarries begun in the Park yielded only inferior stone and eventually stone had to be brought from more distant Taynton and Burford with some even from Plymouth and Ross on Wye. Bringing stone along unsuitable roads by carters who could be very reluctant on muddy winter days or during busy farming seasons inevitably raised the building costs. Any increase in the cost of the works created anxiety for, and complaints from, Sarah.

Soon Sarah reported to the Duke that progress was not as she would expect and she herself had to go to the new site and sort out the details with Vanbrugh. Her inability to trust what was happening, especially in relation to expenditure, resulted in her becoming totally immersed in the building project although she had no professional knowledge nor previous experience of house building. She tried to make day-to-day decisions herself, arguing endlessly with Vanbrugh over the deployment of workmen and materials and the wrong, as she thought, siting of some constructions. She commanded that some parts of the new buildings be demolished and rebuilt in other positions but her main complaints were about money – the waste of money and resources. The Duke's duties in Europe as the Queen's Captain General meant he spent little time in England and that time was usually in the dreary winter months.

Green makes the interesting comment that perhaps it was as well that the robust young Vanbrugh was chosen as architect rather than the elderly, more tractable, Wren who might have had great difficulty dealing with Sarah's determination to avoid all extravagance and to control everything. We should have ended up today with a very different and, in all likelihood, less magnificent building. If Wren had abandoned the project out of inability to fight Sarah we might even have had an incomplete palace on one side of the Glyme and the ruin of another on the other side. As it was Vanbrugh battled on with Sarah for longer than most would have endured and to a stage when his *'owne child'* could grow without his involvement. The arguments were legendary and gave Sarah the reputation of intolerance and meanness which was probably exaggerated. Over this time the relationship between Queen Anne and Sarah was deteriorating. Anne expected long hours of companionship from her female attendants.

Remains of Henry II's Palace as it stood in Woodstock Park in 1714

Elizabeth I when Princess

(*Far left*)
Sir Henry Lee – Master of the Game, Parker and Lieutenant of the Park

(*Left*)
Sir Thomas Parry – Comptroller of the Household to Princess Elizabeth

(*Below*)
Front page of the Charles II Charter of the Borough of Woodstock

High Lodge in 1709 where the Marlboroughs lived while awaiting completion of the east wing in the main building

Column of Victory with the landscape under construction – looking south back to Blenheim Palace

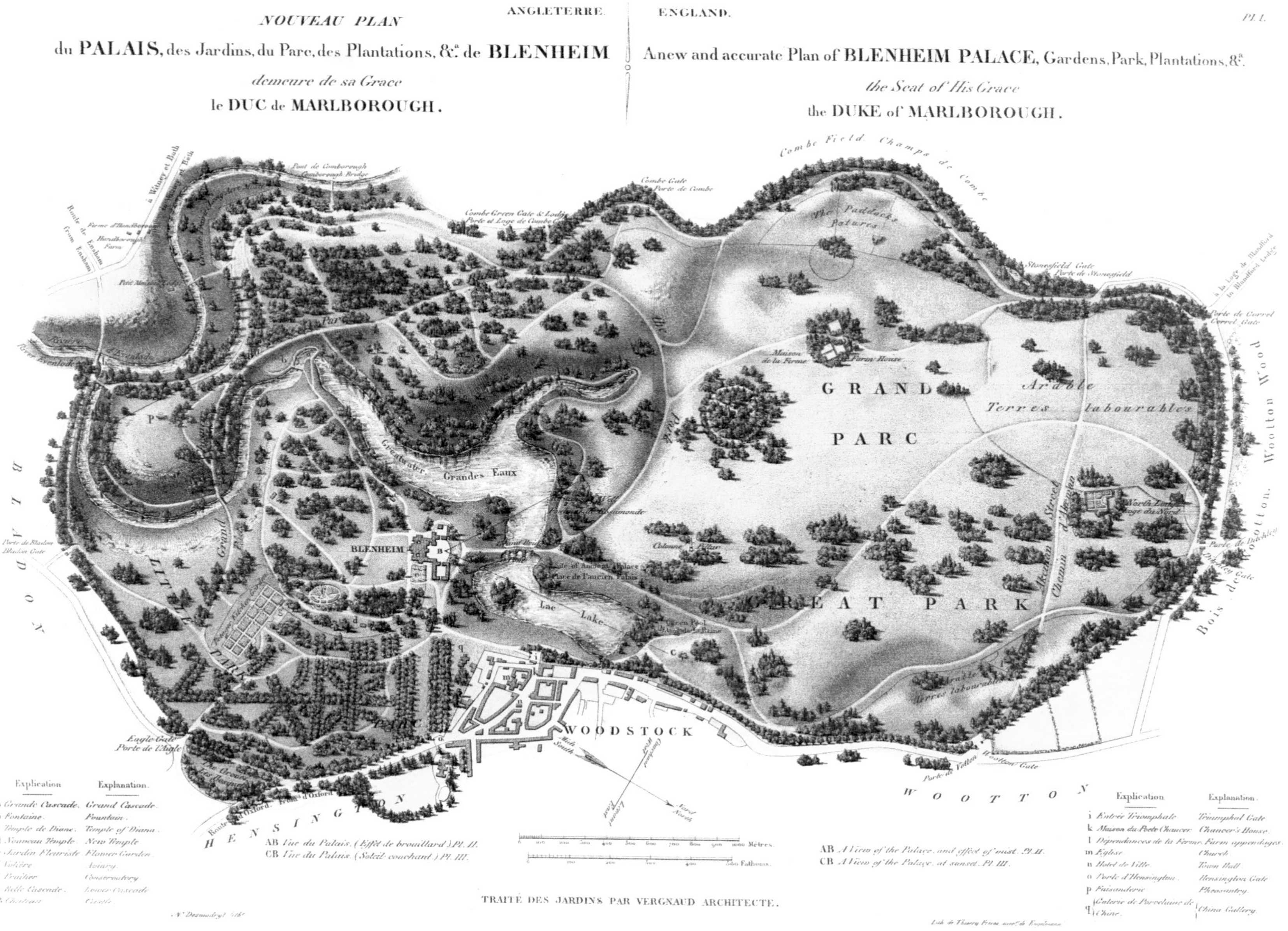

ANGLETERRE. | ENGLAND.

NOUVEAU PLAN

du **PALAIS**, des Jardins, du Parc, des Plantations, &c.ª de **BLENHEIM**

demeure de sa Grace

le **DUC** de **MARLBOROUGH**.

Anew and accurate Plan of **BLENHEIM PALACE**, Gardens, Park, Plantations, &c.ª

the Seat of His Grace

the **DUKE** of **MARLBOROUGH**.

	Explication	Explanation.
a	*Grande Cascade.*	*Grand Cascade.*
b	*Fontaine.*	*Fountain.*
c	*Temple de Diane.*	*Temple of Diana.*
d	*Nouveau Temple.*	*New Temple.*
e	*Jardin Fleuriste.*	*Flower Garden.*
f	*Volière.*	*Aviary.*
g	*Fruitier.*	*Conservatory.*
h	*Belle Cascade.*	*Lower Cascade.*
B	*Château.*	*Castle.*

AB *Vue du Palais, (Effet de brouillard) Pl. II.*
CB *Vue du Palais. (Soleil couchant) Pl. III.*

AB *A View of the Palace, and effect of mist. Pl. II.*
CB *A View of the Palace, at sunset. Pl. III.*

	Explication	Explanation.
i	*Entrée Triomphale.*	*Triumphal Gate.*
k	*Maison du Poete Chaucer.*	*Chaucer's House.*
l	*Dependances de la Ferme.*	*Farm appendages.*
m	*Eglise.*	*Church.*
n	*Hotel de Ville.*	*Town Hall.*
o	*Porte d'Hensington.*	*Hensington Gate.*
p	*Faisanderie.*	*Pheasantry.*
q	*Galerie de Porcelaine de Chine.*	*China Gallery.*

0 100 200 300 400 500 600 700 800 900 1000 Mètres.
0 100 200 300 400 500 Fathoms.

TRAITÉ DES JARDINS PAR VERGNAUD ARCHITECTE.

N. Desmadryl lith.

Lith. de Thierry Frères succ.rs de Engelmann

A new and accurate plan of Blenheim Palace Gardens, Park and Plantations

A 14th-century illustration showing King John riding in the hunt with his dogs

The new heronry now well established on Queen Elizabeth's Island

Bluebells in the glades found in High Park

Woodland fungi found in abundance

Moorhen nest by the lake

Bumble Bees at work

Queen Elizabeth's Island with the original Manor House site on the left and Woodstock Gate on the right

(*Left*)
Migratory birds gathering on the timber causeway with New Woodstock in the background

(*Below, left to right*)
Autumn colours in Woodstock Park

Canada Geese frequent visitors

Clumps of Copper Beech trees planted by the Ninth Duke just below New Bridge

The Stonesfield Tapestry. 'The vast needlework made by a local resident recording the beautiful tessellated pavement in a Roman villa excavated nearby in the early 18th century'

A painting by Turner of Oxford of Wootton village viewed from Top Lane and looking north over West End Ford *c.*1833

View from Old Woodstock, watercolour by the architect John Buckler, 1823

She demanded, for example, that they play cards with her far into the night. Sarah had introduced an impoverished relation Abigail Hill into Anne's household as lady's maid. By 1705 Abigail had acquired an influence of her own with the Queen and eventually usurped Sarah's position in the Royal Household. In 1707 Sarah had a major quarrel with her friend the Queen and lost her job. It is to Queen Anne's credit that she did not then and there, or later when she sacked Marlborough, 'pull the plug' on the whole Blenheim project.

TROUBLESOME TIMES

Money from Parliament did not come on a regular basis. In 1710 Sarah ordered all work to cease until more money was sanctioned by the Treasury. Around this time, Godolphin who was financial overseer of the project and responsible for funds for paying workmen as well as father in law to the Marlborough's daughter Henrietta, was replaced as Lord Treasurer by Edward Harley, First Earl of Oxford and political enemy of the Marlboroughs. This must have been a sickening blow to the people of Woodstock who had benefitted directly from employment opportunities generated by the building work (there were up to 1500 workmen on the site in the early busy years); from numerous non-local men employed and accommodated in the area; and from visitors wanting to see the developing Castle, now more appropriately described as a Palace. Parliament sent Mr Travers MP to review the situation of workers who by then were used to very irregular payment and were often indebted to Woodstock merchants. Travers was so impressed by the situation of unpaid, unemployed, starving, workmen unable to buy food to feed themselves and unable to buy transport home that he borrowed £300 there and then so he could resolve the immediate problems. In 1712 work stopped completely as the Marlboroughs went into exile in The Hague to escape charges of corruption brought by the Duke's long-standing enemies.

The Marlborough's son-in-law, now Lord Godolphin, remained and in 1713 was confronted by an election with Woodstock full of unpaid and now unemployed workmen. Vanbrugh had hit problems earlier with a letter to the Mayor of Woodstock stating that the persecution suffered by the Duke from Queen and Parliament had prevented him paving the town streets. Sarah blamed Vanbrugh's bad spelling on the fact that the letter was sent to a *Major*, not to the *Mayor*, and found its way to the Earl of Oxford and the Queen. Vanbrugh was removed from a number of his national positions and the Queen declared she had done with him. The Mayor of Woodstock was both upset by this disaster and disturbed by the Tories rallying support for the forthcoming election in Woodstock with a meeting at the Rose and Crown. Only freemen could vote so the Mayor suddenly made twenty-five new honorary freemen and Godolphin determined both to pave Woodstock with only freemen as workmen and to employ only freemen in Blenheim garden. Vanbrugh had already produced plans for pavings which sloped gently from the houses towards a central drain and the work was stretched out over seven months – until the election. Green tells us that *'everyone who had handled the paving stones of Woodstock turned out to be Whig to a man'.*

FAREWELL TO VANBRUGH

After Anne's death in 1714 Marlborough and Sarah returned from their exile in The Hague and work began again. Sarah's anger erupted more violently than ever when she discovered in 1716 that Vanbrugh had been living in the gatehouse of the Old Manor House and had used workmen to refurbish the place. He claimed that he had been offered the accommodation by Godolphin when Sarah was out of the country and that living in the Manor House enabled him to oversee the building works more effectively. Vanbrugh had long held out against the Marlboroughs', particularly Sarah's, wish that the Manor House should be demolished. He had written at length about how the Manor House would make *'one of the Most Agreeable Objects that the best of Landskip Painters could invent'*. He even produced a drawing to try to convince his employers of this. Sadly that drawing has disappeared. However, far from supporting the idea of preserving the Manor House, Sarah ordered yet again demolition of all the walls and gatehouse of Henry II's building. If all this had happened only 50 years later, changed ideas about ruins and landscape would have valued the ruins and we might still have remnants of that remarkable building. Did Sarah realise that for some years Vanbrugh had been conducting a pantomime whereby workmen would destroy useless bits of the Manor outbuildings when she was around but when she was absent he would organise repair of the more habitable portions? The Manor House did eventually go. The last of the structure was demolished in 1723.

Since 1709 the family had been living at a renovated High Lodge awaiting completion of the east wing of the main building. They eventually moved into the Palace in 1719. By then Queen Anne had been dead for five years and Vanbrugh had finally resigned three years previously. Sarah had written a long diatribe against her architect to Brigadier General Richards who supervised the waterworks at Blenheim and was Vanbrugh's friend. This was the final straw and Vanbrugh resigned. He never saw inside the building again – Sarah ensured that. When he visited Woodstock with the Duke of Carlisle and family in 1725 he was refused permission to enter the Park by the gateman who had been instructed never to let him in. Poor Vanbrugh had to content himself with peeping over the wall from Old Woodstock and then visiting his friend Dr Cox at the Rectory where he could again look over the wall into the Park at the water and '*some of the other works*'.

FINISHING THE PALACE AND PARK

The Duke had been in poor health for some time and in May 1716 he had a stroke from which he never really recovered. In 1722, after years of ill health and with work on the Palace finally nearing completion, the Duke died and was buried with great pomp and circumstance in Westminster Abbey.

Meanwhile the Duchess had inherited Blenheim and the Royal Park of Woodstock for her lifetime, under the terms of Queen Anne's gift. She was determined to ensure that the memory of her late husband would be preserved for good. Nicholas Hawksmoor returned as architect, designing

Triumphal Arch, Woodstock Town Gate designed by Nicholas Hawksmoor 1723

the imposing stone-arched Town Gate with inscriptions of the Duke's bravery in both Latin and English. It is said that the Duchess had wanted the main entrance to the Palace to be from the Oxford Road at the site of the present Hensington Gate but a resident there flatly refused to move and the plan was abandoned. How then to position the Town Gate? The previous entrance to the Park from the town had probably gone straight out at the end of Park Street by Chaucer's house. By building a high wall at the end of Park Street and setting the gate around a corner from the town, the view of Palace and Park is only seen as one goes through the gate. The effect is dramatic.

Hawksmoor also designed the memorial column which was erected about five years later on the long north avenue to a modified design. A fine gate with tall columns decorated by Grinling Gibbons, known as the Hensington Gate, took the place of the previously anticipated main entrance there. Although the southern part of the wall around the Palace grounds was never completed and the Grand Bridge never did have its intended tall superstructure, the upper lake (called Queen Pool after Queen Philippa, mother of the Black Prince) remained above the old causeway which used to serve the Manor House. A canal ran under the grand bridge with the water level raised by a dam to create a further lake at the west end of the canal.

Sarah had controlled all that happened at Blenheim. Her grandson and heir, whom she considered profligate and a wastrel, was not given the opportunity to live there nor to influence Sarah's running of the estate. The First Duke had acquired land outside the original walls of the Park and

View of the formal canal scheme designed by Armstrong

this brought in considerable income from the rents paid by tenant farmers and villagers and by townsmen who paid annually for hay and grazing rights in the manors the Duke controlled but Sarah found the Palace expensive to maintain, cold and unwelcoming. She spent much of her time away from Blenheim building her new house and garden in Wimbledon.

Sarah, First Duchess of Marlborough, died in 1744 at the age of 78. After her death the Duke's body was brought back to Blenheim where he and Sarah were laid to rest together under Rysbrack's monument in the palace chapel. Because the Marlborough's son had died of smallpox at Cambridge in 1703 Queen Anne had decreed that the Dukedom could be passed on through the female line. The Marlborough's eldest daughter Henrietta was dead. Both Henrietta's son and the first son of Anne, Sarah's second daughter, died without issue before their grandmother. So Charles Spencer, Anne's second son, inherited the title as the Third Duke of Marlborough. His younger brother was John Spencer from whom the Earls of Spencer (and Princess Diana) descend.

CAPABILITY BROWN AT BLENHEIM

The planned Palace and Park were complete when Charles inherited the estate. Few changes took place in the Park until the sons of the Fourth Duke and a Mr Lancelot Brown met at Eton. This led to a chance friendship between the Duke and Mr Brown which was to prove very significant.

The Park had many splendid features but lacked cohesion. Once the Fourth Duke inherited the estate in 1758, he commissioned Lancelot 'Capability' Brown, aged about 46 years and at the height of his career and ability, to envisage one overall plan for the Park. Brown drew together the existing features by radically altering the slopes and contours of the ground to lead the eye from one point to another. He planted trees to link features, to hide features or to create vistas between the clumps. The long term replanting scheme of the late 20th century aims to recover Brown's lost vistas after the Ninth Duke had planted new trees but in the wrong places. He maximised the effect of the river by raising the water level to form large lakes either side of Vanbrugh's Grand Bridge with a dam at the south end disguised as a cascade. Raising the water level by about 16 feet submerged the former canal, the line of which could be seen from the air during the very dry summer of 1976. Brown used the stone and rubble from the old Manor House to support the lower stonework of the bridge before it was submerged. This action finally removed any of the remaining

The Cascade today at the end of the Lake

rubble from Henry II's old manor and Fair Rosamund's Bower. Brown also lowered the hillside above the Glyme to achieve the gentle slopes and curves he wished to create.

At the same time High Lodge which had been home for the King's Ranger and Keeper of the Royal Park (although originally much closer to the Manor House) and home for the Marlboroughs during construction of the Palace, was rebuilt as a gothic folly with tower and castellations. A new bridge south of the Cascade and Pleasure Gardens with Temples to Diana, Flora and Health were constructed. Plans to disguise Park Farm behind a long gothic façade and to build an elaborate gothic bathing house at Rosamund's Well were never implemented.

WOODSTOCK, BLENHEIM AND THE TOURIST TRADE

Over the years work on the Palace and grounds had given Woodstock and some of the villages surrounding the Park new life and some prosperity. The gloving and cut steel jewellery trades profited from tourists visiting Blenheim. Many of the houses had fronted their medieval rough stone walls with ashlar stone which Sarah suspected sometimes came unofficially from the Palace. One such house in Park Street belonged to a 'haberdasher of hats' Symon Hatley who craftily began to rebuild his house at numbers 6–8 in 1704. This, together with other property he acquired, was left to his sailor son when he died in 1712. The sailor son, Simon Hatley, is of some literary significance: south of Cape Horn in October 1719 his boat, the *Speedwell* was followed for some days by a dark-mantled sooty albatross. Hatley was prone to drunkenness and depression. After the albatross had hovered around the ship for some days he shot it *'hoping for better weather thereby'* or so his captain records. The episode is described in Shelvock's *Voyage around the World* which was reading material for the young Samuel Taylor Coleridge.

The work carried out by the Fourth Duke in the Palace grounds also encouraged the local economy. The role of the Park as a deer park had diminished greatly and horse racing had almost ceased after 1734 but the Palace grounds were attracting not only other nobility but ordinary travellers.

A page from the *New Guide to Blenheim*, written in 1789 by the Reverend William Mavor states that *'Blenheim may be seen every afternoon from three to five o'clock, except on Sundays and public days ... . The Park and Gardens, on proper application, will be shewn at any hour of the day, except during the time of Divine Service on Sundays'*. What drew visitors to Blenheim was the effect created by the very extensive and labour intensive work of Capability Brown – an effect which remains today in the *'striking grandeur'* described by Neale in 1823. An enthusiastic Daniel Defoe visiting in 1724 was

The New Bridge south of the Cascade designed by William Chambers, 1772/73

'The finest view in England' as expressed by Lord Randolph Spencer Churchill

uncertain whether the lustre of the building added more to the country round than the lustre of the country added to the building. He was very clear that to him the whole site was *'a monument to the generous temperament of the English nation; who in so glorious a manner rewarded the services of those who acted for them as he* [Marlborough] *did'*. Mavor called the place *'one of the most enchanting prospects in nature'*. Today, for those entering the Park by the Town Gate from Woodstock, the view still echoes the words of Lord Randolf Spencer Churchill that this is *'the finest view in England'*.

The diarist John Byng, writing in his *Rides round Britain* in July 1785, gives vivid accounts of life in Woodstock and the Park. He enjoyed driving in the phaeton from Oxford to Woodstock; ordering dinner at The Bear; checking progress in the construction of the new tower at St Mary Magdalene Church; then sauntering about the Park: *'a charming forest and country with many packs of hounds'*. He was shown around by Mr Cross, landlord of The Bear and a park keeper and commented that the island in the lake had been part of the old causeway which formerly served the old Manor House and that the old oaks were rapidly decaying and in need of replacement. On a second visit in August 1787 he stayed at the Bear again. Having a quiet time reading about the Duke's exploits from the memorial plaques in the Park and listening to the sound of two French horns coming from the Palace, he commented that *'The worst thing about Blenheim is the vicinity of the town, whence come externally all the horrid noises of dogs, bells, etc., etc'.* He found the Duke's menagerie shabby although there were some interesting species of deer and a Spanish ass for breeding purposes. There were fifty gardeners under the Head Gardener Mr Shipley and another 100 people employed in the Park. Young pheasants abounded in the rearing coops. Fishing in the lake and streams was good and included 'trolling' or bottom-fishing for pike and such like.

The Bear Hotel, Woodstock where John Byng stayed when passing through the county

BACK TO THE WALL

Along with his other changes to the Park, the Fourth Duke purchased land in Hensington which had once belonged to the Knights Templars but had had many owners since. Once again the Park was extended. Henry I's seven-mile stone wall was now eleven miles in length, the length that it remains today nine hundred years after it was first built.

6 *Woodstock Crafts and Trades*

JOHN BANBURY · CAROL ANDERSON

WOODSTOCK has always been a small town. In its early days the demands of the royal household and the court based on the Manor House promoted trade in the area. In the 13th century the town could claim ironmongers, dyers, harpers, nappers, parchmyers, wymplers, tailors, carpenters, tanners, turners, smiths, weavers, potters, chapmen, parkers and marshals for the park. Foresters and woodsmen also lived in the communities around the park.

The charter from King Henry VI in 1453 confirmed existing established markets and fairs in Woodstock and also permitted local inhabitants to control trade and prices of items such as bread and leather products. Only members of the merchant guild could trade within the town. As in most communities, specific crafts in Woodstock derived from need and the facilities available. Bell founding, cut steel jewellery and glove making are the trades for which the town is best remembered and which have left their artefacts around the country.

BELL FOUNDING

Very little is recorded about the bell founders and their foundries in Woodstock. We know more or less nothing about where their workshops were situated. Yet there are examples of church bells in towers around Oxfordshire and in neighbouring counties made in Woodstock in the 18th century and still ringing today. The lack of information about bell founding in the town may relate to the short life (about 60 years) of the craft at a time when few could read or write. If written records were made, they have not survived.

Keene is the family name associated with bell founding in Woodstock. James Keene's name is associated with property at what is now the

Images of the Crafts & Trades for which Woodstock was renowned

Punchbowl Inn in Oxford Street. As this property had belonged to Cornwell's grammar school between 1602 and 1923, Keene was probably renting the property. He was known to have established a bell foundry in the town sometime in the late 1620s. Woodstock Borough papers record that in 1628 James Keene, wishing to become a freeman of the Borough so that he could trade in the town, agreed to cast a bell in part payment for his freedom. The cost of purchasing freedom of the Borough was five pounds but this could be reduced in exchange for services rendered. Keene paid thirty shillings. In 1626 a Mary Keene had left a legacy of twenty pounds to the Corporation charity a part of which was recorded as being taken up in 1628. As freedom to trade was usually confined to residents of the town, was Mary a close relative with whom James may have been staying before he received his freedom? We do not know.

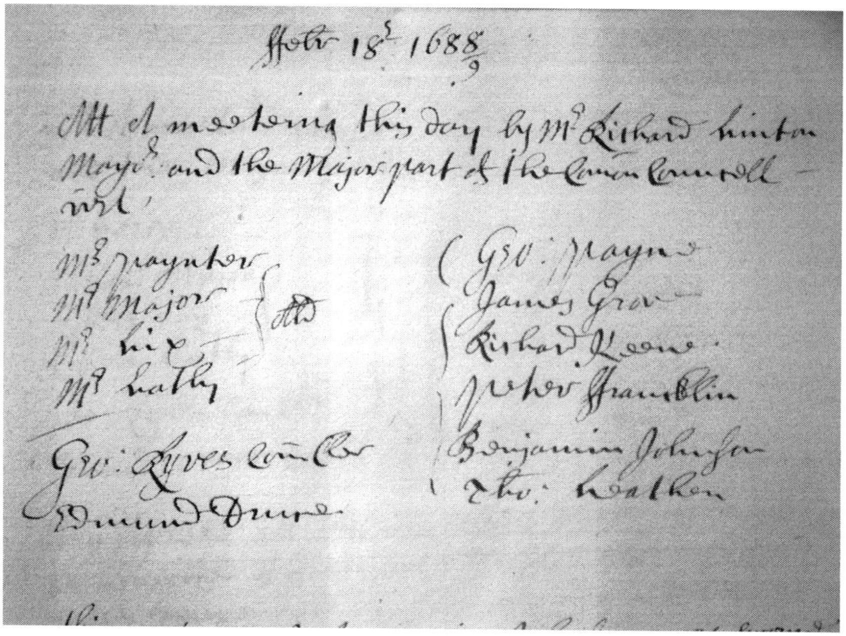

ffebr 18th 1688/9

Att A meeting this day by Mr Richard hinton Mayor and the Major part of the Comon Councell viz

Mr Paynter
Mr Major
Mr hix
Mr hatly

Geo: Payne
James Grove
Richard Keene
Peter ffranklin
Benjamin Johnson
Tho: heathen

Geo: Ryves Com Clr
Edmund Drure

Richard Keene attendance at the Borough Council meeting 1688

James would have had to be trained before setting up his own business. His father, a Richard Keene coming from somewhere near Steeple Aston, was mentioned as having made alterations to the bells at Christchurch Cathedral in Oxford. 'Alterations' may imply working on the hanging of the bells rather than making them. Nevertheless James could have learnt his craft from his father.

Keene family members occupied several properties in the town. A Richard Keene was a tenant in what had previously been the Bull Inn in Market Street but which was probably residential by the late 17th century. Yet we do not know where the bell foundry was located. A barn and chimney now the kitchen of an old cottage in Union Street might have been the workshop and chimney as the present owners found a pit in the shape of a bell whilst clearing their garden. This might have been a mould in which the Keenes cast their bells. The next door house, although new, is called 'Bell Cottage'. Does this reflect the informative name of some previous dwelling here?

Only the old bells inscribed by members of the Keene family provide any information about the output of the foundry. In the seventeenth century St Mary Magdalene's Church in Woodstock had three bells which were repaired or recast by James Keene in 1633. A treble and a tenor bell which probably came from Keene's foundry were added in 1662 and 1666 respectively. The Keene family also supplied the fourth and fifth bells for King's Sutton Church in 1626 since both bells bear the inscribed name of James Keene. Likewise James Keene's name is on the sixth bell in Thame Church, cast in 1664, and the first and second bells in Holywell Church made in 1677. It is not always James Keene though. Five of the bells in the Carfax Church tower in Oxford were marked '*Richardus Keene me fecit. 1676*'. Was this Richard James' father, his brother or his son? It seems unlikely to have been his father so late in the century. Richard Keene's name also appears on the fifth bell at St Michael's in Oxford, with the date 1668 and in 1680 Richard Keene was brought in to tune the ring of bells at St. Mary's in Woodstock.

Correspondence from Reverend Harold Goddard dated January 1984, states that the Worcester village of Martley is very proud of its peal of six bells, thought to be the oldest complete ring in the country. These were cast by Richard Keene in 1673. In 1983 they were taken down and sent to Whitechapel for retuning. They were re-hung on a new frame in Martley Church Tower at a cost of over £15,000.

Mr Lukas, in his 1857 *Account of Church Bells,* states that the foundry in Woodstock closed in 1681. Was he right? A Borough Council meeting in 1688 records Richard Keene's signature. Some of the bells described above post-date 1681 and a bell ascribed to Richard Keene was cast for the church at Stow on the Wold in 1686.

Woodstock carillon. Unfortunately the Keene bells do not survive at Woodstock's St Mary Magdalene. The five bells were recast into six bells by William and Henry Bagley in 1708 with a donation of £100 from the First Duke of Marlborough. In 1786 these six bells were placed in the newly rebuilt church tower and two new bells added by the Fourth Duke making a peal of eight bells. A new church clock by John Briant of Hertford was installed in 1792 together with a new chiming mechanism, which played six times in 24 hours with a different tune for each day of the week. The tunes were chosen by the Woodstock Corporation and are the same as are played today. Robb Smith describes them as popular hits of the day for the late

Richard 'KEENE CAST THIS RINGE 1673' for St Peter's Church in Martley

The inscription is cast on No.5 bell at St Peter's Church, Martley

eighteenth century. The mechanism had to be wound twice a day by climbing the narrow winding stairs to the clock loft. This procedure continued until 1940 when the ban on church bells in anticipation of enemy invasion silenced church towers across the country.

John Briant's original hand-wound mechanism was replaced by an electric machine in 1956. A plaque by the doorway to the church tower records the restoration which was carried out to celebrate Woodstock's Charter quincentenery and Queen Elizabeth II's coronation in 1953. Woodstocks from across the world contributed towards the restoration, by John Smith of Derby, which reproduces the seven different tunes played by the original 1792 carillon. These are:

Sunday *'Hanover'* – a tune originally for the 104th psalm and now often used for 'Oh worship the King'.

Monday *'Marriage Vow'* – source unknown.

Tuesday *'Happy Clown'* – first published in 1718 and included in The Beggar's Opera but later becoming a popular song under this name.

Wednesday *'Malbrouck s'en va-t-en guerre'*. Robb Smith suggests this was sung by a French soldier at the Battle of Malplaquet in 1709 and then later by a Flemish nurse to Marie Antoinette's son. It is the equivalent of 'For he's a jolly good fellow'.

Thursday *'Highland Laddie'* – this was set to a Robbie Burns song 'I hae been at Crookieden'.

Friday *'Marionette'* – apparently this was known locally as 'I'll tell daddy when he comes home'.

Saturday *'Haunted Tower'* – this was from Stephen Storace's 1789 opera 'The Haunted Tower'. (Stephen and his sister Nancy knew Mozart well and Nancy sang Susannah in the first performance of *The Marriage of Figaro*.)

The present machinery has been recently serviced and repaired and the carillon still sounds at 9am, 1pm, 5pm and 9pm each day.

WOODSTOCK CUT STEEL

The building of Blenheim Palace in the early 18th century brought prosperity to the town and Woodstock craftsmen began to gain a reputation for making high quality cut steel products apparently using horseshoe nails as their raw material. Visitors to the Palace, both fashionable guests and sightseers, provided a ready market for these goods and helped to spread the steelworkers' reputation nationally and ultimately internationally. Writing in 1750, Madame Bocage, a French traveller, observed that *'The English have brought the art of polished steel to perfection. At Woodstock are to be seen masterpieces of this sort of workmanship.'*

Despite suggestions to the contrary there is no certain reference to steel work in Woodstock before the early 18th century. The craft's introduction to Woodstock was attributed locally to a whitesmith, Henry Metcalfe, who bought his freedom as a gunsmith in 1715 and by 1718 was taking apprentices as a whitesmith. His son Henry called himself a whitesmith and polished steelworker. Together the Metcalfes took on at least 15 apprentices between 1718 and 1776, the earliest being George Eldridge who became a master himself in 1734 and later one of the town's principal steelworkers. Eldridge's son, also George, became 'steel jeweller' to Queen Charlotte, wife of George III.

The craft appears to have remained in the hands of relatively few families. Other masters included Alderman Thomas Grantham grocer and steelworker, his son Thomas and two of their apprentices: Thomas Wyatt and William Harrison. William Kerwood was apprenticed to George Eldridge in 1743 and his son Robert was also a steelworker. A listing of tradesmen in the town in 1790 also includes a Richard Taylor as a steelmaker. At its height in 1768 the steel industry employed 20–30 hands, journeymen earning between 15 shillings and 2 guineas a week when, by comparison, men and women making gloves were earning between eight and nine shillings.

In the 18th century good quality steel was very expensive to manufacture and its use was largely confined to high-value specialty products such as swords and precision instruments. The strength and malleability of steel did, however, make it an ideal material for the production of the intricately crafted objects of personal adornment made by the Woodstock steelworkers.

Woodstock steel also had a reputation for requiring little polishing to retain its lustre. It was even said that the steel was 'stainless' and did not

Polished cut steel jewellery

require polishing. This, a century and more before the production of stainless steel, suggests that the steel used in the manufacture of these items possessed distinctive qualities. The secret appears to have been in the source of the steel used in the town. Writing in 1813, Brewer, in his history of the town, states that in Woodstock: *'The articles of polished steel are entirely made from the old nails of horses' shoes, which are formed into small bars, before being applied to the various purposes of delicate workmanship'*. The preferred nails were those made from Swedish steel which, with its high copper content, was easy to work but strong. In the hands of the highly skilled Woodstock craftsmen this scrap was converted into *'articles of infinitely greater price, according to their weight than purest gold'*.

Little evidence survives to explain how the cut steel items were made but in October 1753 a Swedish metallurgist, Reinhold Rutger Angerstein visited the town to gather information about the steel factories there. In his account he provides a description of the manufacturing process. He observes that *'most of the work ... is carried out when the material is still in the form of soft iron, subsequently it is packed in paste and case hardened. Care is taken to complete all the work as far as possible before the case-hardening takes place and that includes a fair amount of polishing, which makes the final polishing so much easier. The packed box is covered with an iron lid and placed in the hearth, in which the fire has been blown up to a high temperature. The lid is made with a little handle so that it can be lifted up for checking the heat inside. The temperature has reached its proper level when the black material of the paste is white all over. The box is then removed from the fire and the contents thrown into a cauldron full of water. A sample piece, dimensioned in accordance with the articles in the bath, is also placed in the box and subsequently fractured to show how far the hardening has penetrated, if it has gone too far or not far enough. When making the Diamanté objects the steel diamonds are screwed into place and the whole job is completed, but then taken apart especially for the case-hardening and polishing'.*

Given the small scale nature of the industry it is most probable that manufacture was carried out in workshops or small warehouses somewhere close to the master's house, possibly in the backyards of their properties which clustered around the centre of the town. The Eldridges were a family of ironmongers with premises behind the Town Hall and quantities of steel dross are said to have been found in the garden of this and the adjoining property.

Another suggested site of manufacture is in what is now the Feathers Hotel, where a quantity of steel filings are said to have been found. No steel forges are marked on early maps and there is no other documentary evidence to help in the search for sites of manufacture.

The Woodstock craftsmen created distinctive, highly polished, studded jewellery and objects such as watch-chains, buckles, scissors, buttons, boxes, chatelaines and, more rarely, swords. Although cut steel was made elsewhere in England, what sets the products of the Woodstock workshops apart is the quality of the workmanship particularly on the guards of swords and on chatelaines where elegantly executed plant and floral motifs dominate the decorative design. *The comparison of the workmanship of a laced and plaited ruff to the laboured nicety of the steel-work of Woodstock is just'.* The distinctive cut-steel studs used by the Woodstock craftsmen were fully screwed rather than riveted and could therefore be removed for cleaning. The products of the town's workshops were unique in this respect. Other centres of manufacture such as Birmingham did not indulge in such time-consuming niceties. *'Steel goods and gloves are the two staples of Woodstock. Their watch-chains, sword hilts ... are more highly polished and better standard than those of Birmingham. They polish all with the hand.*

Quality of workmanship shown in the detail of this sword guard

Their studs screw, and everything can be taken to pieces and cleaned whereas the Birmingham studs are riveted.' The studs used in Woodstock made pieces were also cut with a concave diamond facet which increased the reflected light and made the finished pieces sparkle like diamonds in candle-light.

With a few notable exceptions, such as a pair of scissors in the collections of the Victoria and Albert Museum stamped with the initials GE (presumably for George Eldridge), most Woodstock cut steel does not bear marks which identify its origins or which enable particular pieces to be attributed to the masters working in the town. The majority of pieces can be attributed to the Woodstock craftsmen only on the basis of the quality of their design and manufacture.

In their comparatively short history the products of the Woodstock workshops achieved not only a national reputation but one which extended throughout Europe. The opening of a Woodstock stage wagon service to London in 1773 and subsequent improvements to the service enabled steelworkers to transport their goods more quickly and easily to London where they were retailed by the leading cutlers and jewellers of the day such as Gray's in Bond Street. In 1742 Horace Walpole sent a box of steel wares from Woodstock to the British Consul in Florence requesting that they be given as diplomatic gifts. In his *'Diary of a Journey to England 1761–2'* Count Friedrich Kielmansegge observed that Woodstock was renowned all over England for fine workmanship in steel and that the best goods in London came from Woodstock. Brewer in the *Topographical and Historical Description of Oxon* recorded that in 1813 a chain weighing only two ounces was sold in France for £170. A box in which the freedom of the Borough was presented to Viscount Cliefdon cost thirty guineas while a garter star made for the Duke of Marlborough fetched fifty guineas.

By the late 18th century, despite better transport to London, the Woodstock industry was finding it increasingly difficult to compete with the prices of goods from cities such as Birmingham, Wolverhampton and Sheffield. Visiting Woodstock in 1778, Mrs Philip Lybbe Powys admired the craftsmanship but complained about the price of a pair of scissors with decorated handles at 15 guineas the pair which she considered to be *'extravagant to a degree, as the steel, they told me is equally good at 2s 6d, the open work above adding to the price'*.

By 1807 competition from mass produced cut steel was being blamed for the collapse of Woodstock's industry which by then employed fewer than a dozen men. In addition, cheap imitation goods in cast iron were being made in Berlin to supply the German states whose access to British manufacture was cut off by the Napoleonic wars. George Eldridge turned to his family's other interest, gloving, and was later called variously ironmonger, brazier, and tin-man.

References in the *Gentleman's Magazine* show that steel was still being manufactured in 1820 but there is no mention of steel at Woodstock after 1850 in the *Gazetteer* published by Fullerton & Co. Local people have said that steel was still being manufactured as late as 1862 but it seems unlikely that there would have been much demand for it as late as that as Birmingham and Sheffield wares produced by machine were cheaper. In 1898 an article in the *Oxford Journal & County News* could record that *'for nearly 100 years the manufacture has ceased'* and even in the Eldridge family the *'recollection of how beautiful chains, scissors, buckles and buttons were made is very vague'*.

GLOVING

The crafts and trades developing early in Woodstock's history would have been influenced by the needs and the patronage of visiting royalty and the court as well as the availability of materials. Deer and sheepskins from both the Park and the Cotswolds encouraged production of the fine leather gloves suitable for the court. Production of fine hand-stitched gloves continued after Blenheim Palace was built when many visitors – tourists – began to visit the town.

Gloves were being made locally in the 13th century. Skins were traded at the Woodstock Fell Market which had its own regulations. A glover is recorded as falling foul of the local regulations in 1415. In 1580 only three people from outside the borough were allowed to trade at the Fell Market.

The glovers worked from their own houses or from workshops set up behind their houses. Producing the fine wash leather for the front and back of the gloves was a skilled but tedious process. The animal skins were washed, tanned and dyed. They were then softened by drawing them backwards and forwards over a metal blade with a dull edge. This was followed by a paring knife to create a uniform thickness. Shears were used in Woodstock to cut the front and back of the glove. The skill was to cut as many gloves as possible out of each skin without wasting leather. Leftover pieces could be used for thumbs or button-holes which were stitched in later.

The glover or his carter took the cut leather 'tranks' to the cottages of individual, predominantly female, workers in Woodstock and surrounding villages. These workers hand stitched the gloves and the carter would return to Woodstock with the sewn gloves for finishing. Thumbs were stitched in, gauntlets sewn on, decoration stitched on the backs and then the gloves were pressed with a wooden roller on a workbench to improve the appearance or ironed on a heated metal hand. Traditionally, once finished and inspected, each pair was tacked together and wrapped in tissue paper. Later, cellophane bags were substituted but the best and most expensive hand-stitched gloves were always packed individually in boxes.

Glove Cutters hard at work – from the left Doug Beckett, Fred Margetts and a 'Chapel man from Charlbury way'

Although Woodstock was famed for the fine quality of its gloves, it did not just produce fine wash leather gloves. In the middle ages heavy buckskin gauntlets were worn by hunters, falconers, horse-riders and those hedging in the Park. Leather breeches were also manufactured in Woodstock as elsewhere in the Cotswolds. Woodstock gloves featured at the 1851 Great Exhibition. Gloves were made for the military in the Civil and Napoleonic wars and World War I. The gloves worn by the Beefeaters at the Tower of London were also made in Woodstock. In the 20th century sports gloves were made for famous cricketers such as Jack Hobbs, horse-riders, drivers and boxers and Woodstock gloves were used in the first production of My Fair Lady.

Queen Elizabeth I had been presented with a pair of gloves on a visit to Oxford in 1556. In 1952 Queen Elizabeth II received an almost identical pair from the town. Over the centuries royalty including James I, assize judges and a wide range of foreign visitors have been presented with Woodstock gloves.

The industrial revolution invented stitching machines for glove making and large glove manufacturers invested in the town's factories from 1850 onwards with increasing mechanisation. Glove production went up but the number of people involved in the trade went down. Whilst the advent of the railway enabled more effective movement of skins into Woodstock and gloves out of Woodstock, trade was beginning to decline.

From the 16th to 19th centuries, many properties in Woodstock were occupied by gloving families. In the 19th century the industry expanded into many buildings used previously for other purposes such as those relinquished by steel makers; the Corporation cockpit; redundant malthouses; even alms houses. In Old Woodstock the Manor Farmhouse was used by glovers and the Glove House was built on the other side of the main road.

In 1850 there were some 100 men and 1500 women employed in the industry although only 85 of the Woodstock population of about 1800 people were employed in gloving and most of these were women sewing gloves in their own homes. The remainder of employees were from the villages, usually homeworkers. Gardner's *Directory of Oxfordshire 1852* estimated that Woodstock produced 7200 pairs of gloves a week. By 1876, Harrod's *Directory* was listing only nine manufacturers most of whom employed between twenty to forty workers in the factory but many women outworkers. Purpose-built factories were beginning to be developed in the town with machinery which speeded up some of the

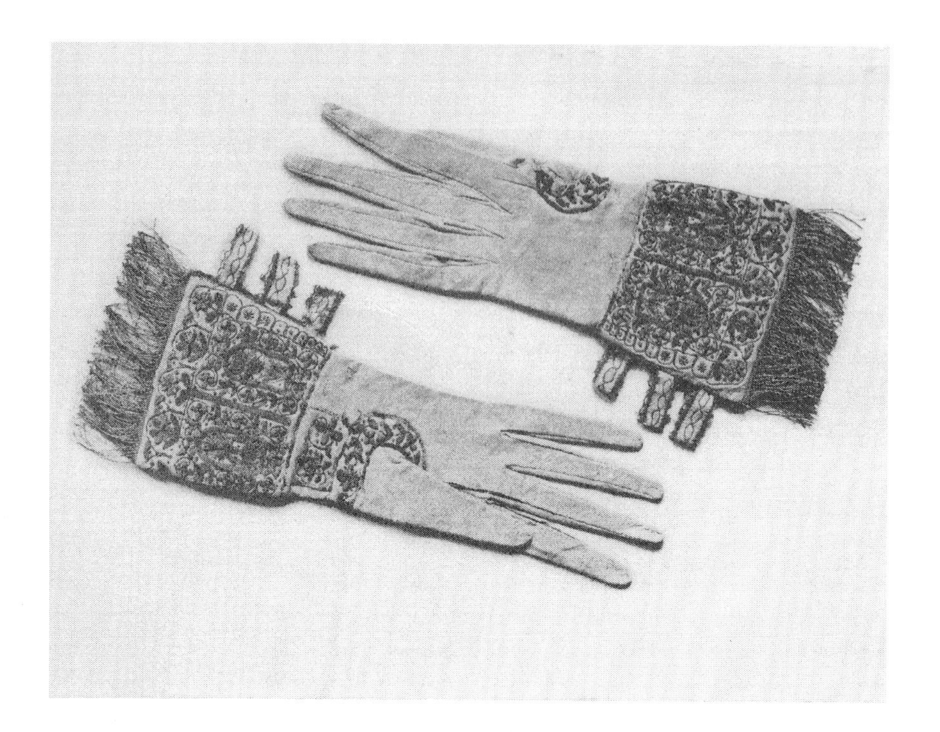

The pair of gloves presented to Queen Elizabeth I in 1556 on a visit to Oxford

Pair of gloves being presented to Queen Elizabeth II by Mayor Alderman C W Banbury on her visit to Woodstock, 8 April 1959

Front view of Messrs. Atherton & Clothier Glove Factory on Oxford Street 1923

otherwise manual work. However the skins still had to be washed and dried on the drying grounds.

By 1918 many well-established Woodstock glove factories had closed. For centuries gloves had been an essential part of dress for both men and women. This was no longer so. Nevertheless, the superior quality of the wash-leather gloves produced in Woodstock meant that mechanised sewing machines did not take all the trade for elegant hand-sewn gloves but they did make it easier to produce large quantities of affordable gloves and thus challenge the home-working industry. By the 1930s all the main factories in Woodstock were owned by, or manufactured for, larger enterprises and only about 200 outworkers remained. By 1966 only thirty-five people were employed in gloving in Woodstock and there were few outworkers. The last factory, Leslie Tubb's Woodstock Leathercraft, which made the high quality hand-made dress gloves for which the town was famous, closed in 1990. Now no gloves are made in Woodstock.

7 The End of the Rotten Borough

JOHN BANBURY · ELIZABETH POSKITT

WOODSTOCK benefitted greatly from the employment offered by the construction and landscaping of Blenheim Palace and Park but the town then went through a period of economic and, in some ways, social decline. The town population had grown only very slowly between the 12th and 17th centuries. The 17th-century population was estimated in the region of 500–700: much the same as that estimated for 1279. Over the 18th century however this increased quite dramatically to 1322 inhabitants in 1801 and 1380 in 1831. From this point onwards, until after World War II, censuses usually recorded falling numbers of Woodstock residents when adjusted for the changes in Borough boundaries.

A falling population in the 19th century suggests there were better jobs elsewhere. Certainly employment opportunities arising from the Industrial Revolution were not apparent in Woodstock. Gloving became more mechanised and this increased productivity but fewer workers were required. Machine worked jewellery from Midland cities led to the disappearance of the Woodstock cut steel industry. Although the railway did eventually come to Woodstock it arrived too late to save these industries and it never had much impact on developments in the town although it provided residents with the opportunity to commute to work elsewhere. This period of economic decline was matched by difficulties in local government.

REPRESENTATION AT PARLIAMENT

Over the years the Marlboroughs did much to help develop the town. The Duke financed the building of the Town Hall in 1766 after the Town Council 'invested' the money they were collecting for the purpose in lottery tickets which, not surprisingly, did not bring in the anticipated revenue. However the town was a typical 'pocket borough' with two MPs who were almost invariably friends or relatives of the Duke. One MP for nearly forty years was Sir Henry Watkin Dashwood of Kirtlington who had huge debts and according to Crossley *'needed the protection of a parliamentary seat'*. In 1832 the constituency was enlarged to prevent it being disenfranchised due to its small population and thereafter it sent only one MP to parliament. However it remained a Tory/Conservative seat with the electorate being encouraged to support the ducal candidates by inducements such as rabbit hunts in the park and the opportunity to travel to the election in a ducal carriage. When the constituency was finally abolished by the Redistribution of Seats Act of 1885, the sitting MP was Lord Randolf Churchill, Winston Churchill's father.

LOCAL POLITICS

Local government was likewise influenced by pressures from the Palace. At the beginning of the 19th century, the Town Council had become a very relaxed body with low attendance at meetings and corrupt practices such as using the proceeds from town property for their own benefit and requesting food, drink or free seats at cock fights as bonuses on top of the rates paid by citizens. Councillors were not democratically elected and by the nineteenth century many were living outside the town, sometimes as far away as London. For all the beneficent actions by successive Dukes to improve the town, there were always pro- and anti-Marlborough factions dividing the Corporation.

Woodstock Councillors had never been noted for their skills in conflict resolution. For example, Shelmerdine points out that in the 16th century Councillors could be fined ten shillings if they *'revyle, miscall or gyve any unfitting, undecent or obprobious words'* to one another. In the early 1800s many Councillors did not turn up to meetings, not surprisingly with so many 'absentee' Councillors who had no interest in the town. Things came to a peak in 1831 when the Duke tried to secure the election of a particular candidate as Recorder. His candidate was voted in when the Council was not quorate and the Town Clerk protested. Stalemate ensued. For eight years the Council did not meet, did no business and essential action was undertaken by the Mayor and the Town Clerk. In 1838 they were finally compelled to meet by a writ of *mandamus* obtained by the grammar school master, fed up with not being paid for five years. Having at last met, the Council elected the Duke's choice of Recorder and got on with their work.

During the time the Council was not meeting, the Municipal Corporations Act of 1835 was passed which might have helped reform local government except that Woodstock was exempted from the Act along with about one hundred other small boroughs and continued to work according to the charter of Charles II. So it was only in 1886, despite earlier attempts of some ratepayers to expose the corruptions by appealing to the Privy Council, that the Corporation was at last brought into line with the Municipal Corporations Act. Old Woodstock and parts of Hensington were incorporated into the new municipal borough.

SOCIAL WORK IN THE COMMUNITY

Before 1886 many Liberals and non conformists viewed the Corporation as unacceptably unrepresentative of the community and supported the community through 'good works' independent of the Corporation. There was plenty of need for social work within the town. Blenheim had brought

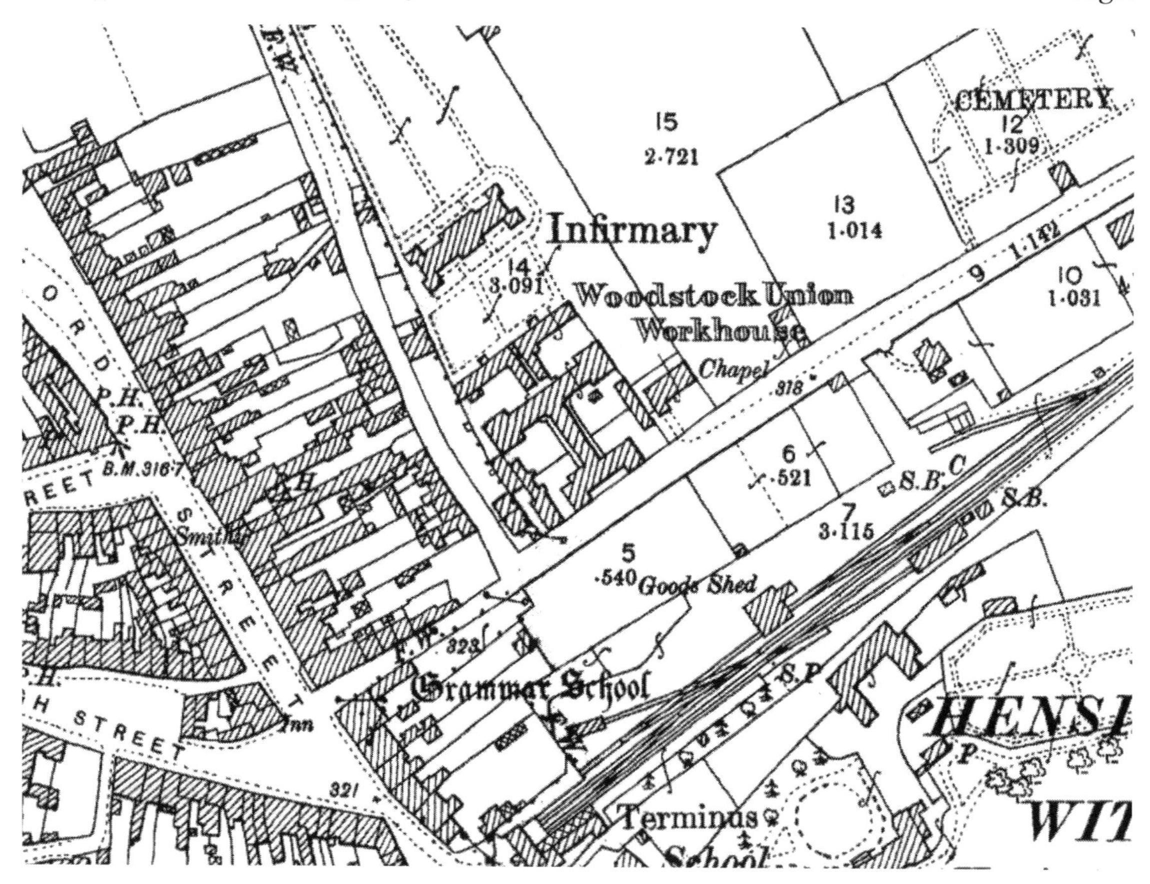

Site Plan showing location of the Union Work House on Hensington Road

Union Work House on Hensington Road built 1836–1837

tourism to Woodstock and an estimated sixteen inns were licensed over most of the 19th century. However many people and families remained poor and uneducated. In such an environment the Victorian social conscience and liberal ideas for the relief of poverty and education for all led to community developments with Church Board and National Schools set up in all the demesne villages usually on land donated by the Duke. After the Poor Law Act of 1834 the parochial workhouse on Oxford Street was replaced by a much larger one, built in Hensington Road by the Poor Law Guardians under the Workhouse Act, with a chapel and hospital as well. The site of this chapel is now marked by the memorial garden in Hensington Road. The name Union Street running off Hensington Road down what was the side of the workhouse refers to the Woodstock Poor Law Union of over thirty parishes which supported and used the work-house. The stories of some of the applications to the Poor Law Union in the 1830s and 1840s illustrate not only the difficulties of rural life for many even into the 20th century but the range of aid offered:

'Sarah Harper with 7 children, of Duns Tew. Husband in Gaol. Earned 8s a week. Receives 3 loaves. One child earns 2s a week. Allowed 12 loaves, the 6 already received to be deducted'

and

'– ordered that the Clerk write ... to know whether the trusses supplied by George Albion of ... are good and such as they can recommend'

but *'James Bayliss of Steeple Barton applies for relief for himself, father and mother. The father says he won't work because he must get up early in the morning and he could not then lie in bed. Dismissed'.*

It is clear that the Union attempted to get fathers who had deserted their families to take responsibility for them and, if not, *'the Overseers of Woodstock proceed against John Huband for refusing to support his children, unless he takes them out of the House tomorrow.'* Where paupers admitted to the workhouse were from other parts of the country there were efforts made to get other Poor Law Unions to take financial responsibility and to accept the pauper into their workhouse. At the same time they were prepared to provide relief in the form of food or clothing for applicants just released from gaol and for illegitimate children. The vestry also helped: *'It was agreed that George Dewsnap, a poor parishioner, at his own desire wishing to emigrate with his wife and family to the United States of America, that the sum necessary for that purpose in the most economical manner be provided by the parish'.*

WOODSTOCK AND BLENHEIM FIRE BRIGADES

When the Fourth Duke organised Sir William Chambers to build the new Town Hall in 1766, he ensured that the design included an engine house to keep the town's fire cart in a central position. The fire cart had been given to the town by James Bertie, later Earl of Abingdon, in 1680 and for the past 200 years freemen had each contributed a leather fire bucket costing five shillings as part of their joining fee. The town had amassed up to 98 buckets. Long ladders and hooks were housed in the church tower as the two churchwardens and the vestry had fire fighting amongst their duties. Corporation and vestry seem to have shared the responsibilities but with the vestry paying for care and upkeep of the cart over much of this time.

1861 the Duke presented the Town with a drinking fountain placed in the wall of the Town Hall

Water for fire fighting could be a problem. Until the 1950s most Oxfordshire villages took their water from their own springs and wells. Woodstock residents not only had their own wells but piped water as well from Blenheim, brought from the Glyme by a pump installed at the mill by the causeway.

This system pumped water into pipes and hydrants in the main streets but water pressure was somewhat low.

In 1861 a large fire at the Palace destroyed the Titian Gallery (although there were reputedly no Titians in the gallery at the time). The Duke showed his gratitude to the town's fire brigade for their help extinguishing the fire by installing a second pump at the mill. Further, with help from the Corporation he installed more water pipes, increased the number of water hydrants and presented the town with a drinking water fountain placed in the wall of the Town Hall where it remains below the stone sundial repositioned on the Town Hall from the old market cross.

The Woodstock Volunteer Fire Brigade had been started in 1872 by a group of businessmen and residents in the town by which time the vestry had transferred responsibility for the fire engine to the union overseers and the Corporation was not prepared to pay to maintain the fire engine. Fearing the possible effect of no fire brigade on their homes and businesses, these men formed a team led by John Banbury, tailor and outfitter, and Stanley Henman, solicitor. They took over maintenance of the fire engine and raised money locally and from the fire insurance companies which had been set up since the Great Fire of London. The Sun, The London and several other companies had local agents and those who contributed to their schemes were given 'fire plaques' to put on their properties, some of which can still be seen on houses in the town. The motive power for the four-wheeled manually operated pump kept at the Town Hall was provided by the carrier's two horses, which, if needed, first had to be

Woodstock Volunteer Fire Brigade with their Manual pump and Bugler 1898

Fire Bell attached to the east wall of the Town Hall

caught from the meadows or fields in Oxford Road or Hensington and brought to the Town Hall to be harnessed to the cart and then driven to the fire. Those requiring the fire brigade called them by tolling a large bell on the eastern wall of the Town Hall.

Blenheim also had a fire brigade manned by the Palace staff with a steamer and a manual pump each drawn by two horses. Led by the enthusiasm of the Duke, Blenheim hosted several fire brigade competitions from the 1890s into the 1930s. Photographs show Woodstock's Volunteer Brigade with their manual pump, two horses and a full crew from many Woodstock families parading at a large international fire brigade competition sponsored by the Duke in 1898. The businesses represented by the brigade included outfitter, draper, baker, solicitor, insurance agent, chimney sweep, grocer and glover.

In 1908 the Woodstock brigade attended a large fire at the church tower in Combe. Doug Margetts, later a retained fireman in Woodstock, was about five-years-old at the time and remembered seeing the horse-drawn fire engine, which had come from Woodstock, arriving and pumping all the water from the village pond in the attempt to quench the fire. The brigade was probably called out by a telephone message from Combe Mill over the new telephone system just installed at the Palace. Even so, the belfry was lost together with all the church records.

Fund-raising enabled the Brigade in 1924 to buy a Model T Ford motor fire engine with ladders, pump, hoses and a fire bell to warn of approach. This was again kept in the Town Hall. It was named the 'John Banbury' after Woodstock's first fire chief. With the back-up of the carrier's van, this Model T fire engine served the brigade well until they were able to purchase a more modern engine in 1933. This was too big to fit into the Town Hall engine house so two cottages in Oxford Street were converted to house it. After 1939 Fletcher's House in Park Street became the County Fire headquarters and was only decommissioned when Kidlington Fire Headquarters opened. Fletcher's House is now the Oxfordshire Museum.

Doug Margetts recalled going round the houses during the war waking up the firemen with a rattle to alert them that they were being called since no bells could be rung during war time. On the night of the Baedeker raid, a very cold night's ride to Coventry on the open side of a fire engine to assist with the fires there, then riding back to Woodstock again on the open engine, did not stop him despite his frozen hands going to work in the glove factory at seven o'clock that morning. Several other long journeys were made during the blitz: to Maidstone, Reading and London with fire fighting around St Paul's Cathedral. The Fire Chief, then CW 'Bill' Banbury, wrote in his notebook of the problems the Woodstock Brigade faced there, through lack of water, as the blitz had taken place at low tide when there was little water in the Thames with which to extinguish fires. On another trip he described a cold and stormy night ride to Plymouth which had been badly bombed. When they arrived the men were frozen on to the bench with ice and had to be melted off with hot water.

In 1941 the government formed the National Fire Service, which absorbed all the auxiliary fire brigades. After the war, the previously independently funded fire brigades were formed into a county-operated structure, funded from the rates. Those in Oxfordshire organised on a part-time basis such as Woodstock were treated as retained brigades and provided with more up-to-date fire stations, equipment and training by the Oxfordshire County Council. Thus the service continues 330 years after the first fire appliance was obtained.

Prizewinning 1924 Fire Brigade with their Model T Ford Motor Fire Engine with ladders, pumps, hoses and a fire bell to warn of approach

Woodstock and Blenheim in the Twentieth Century

ROBERT EDWARDS

THE unprecedented speed of change in Britain in the 20th century is sharply illustrated by the development of Woodstock from 1900 when corn was still cut by hand with scythes on Barn Piece Farm to the almost universal ownership of cars and colour televisions at the Millennium.

POVERTY

In *The Salt of the Earth* Dorothy Calcutt vividly describes the poverty of a huge family in a tied farm cottage in St Andrew's Square, Old Woodstock, at the beginning of the 20th century. She records the overcrowding with twelve people in one small living room/kitchen; the constant struggle to feed the household; the terrible toll of consumption (tuberculosis) which killed children and young adults with awesome regularity. Little girls at the age of twelve left home to become kitchen maids for the middle classes because there was not enough food to go round. Mrs Calcutt's partially sighted aunt walked daily to Eynsham to start hard manual work at 7.30 a.m. Young men walked to the Fenlands to find work.

WOODSTOCK CHARITIES

It is sobering to realise that beneath this farm worker's family there was a further under-class dependent on bread from the municipal charities. There were no pensions and no sick pay. The 1906 *Woodstock Charities Distribution Book* records the weekly delivery of bread to twenty-three adults and twenty-one children to the value of four pence for men, threepence for women, twopence for boys and a penny for girls.

In the same year:

Twelve men received coats
Twelve women received six yards of cloth each to make a dress
Twelve girls had four yards of cloth each for frocks
Eight boys had suits from Strong's at five shillings each
Twenty-one girls received boots at 3s 10d.
Sixteen boys received boots at four shillings a pair
132 people received two hundredweight of coal each

The town's charities were a significant part of the economy. Surplus food from the Duke's table was distributed to the poorest inhabitants. This sounds amazingly condescending but it probably helped some avoid the workhouse.

A picture of Woodstock in the 1920s has been left by the late Mrs Betty Danbury who was born in 1915. She describes going in a starched apron and laced-up boots to school where the children wrote on slates. She recorded:

'Woodstock had more shops years ago: clothes shops, shoe shops, butchers, dairies, paper shops, a printers, a fishmongers, bakers, a fish & chip shop, blacksmiths, doctors, a chemist, watch repairers, cobblers, cafes, pubs, hardware, a tinker, undertakers, sweet shops, private schools, also Church of England boys & girls schools, made a mixed school about 1924, an infant school in Old Woodstock, five glove factories, a Town Hall, a church

View of Town Hall, Market Square and Bear Hotel

hall, a fire engine. We had a Work House with a Home and a Hospital. Also tramps could stop for one night. We had our own Electric works and Gas works. The street lighting was three gas lights, one by the Town Hall, one by the Crown pub and one by the Kings Arms pub. A man used to come up from the Gas works with a 'long arm' to light them. Also an animal market in Park Street of sheep, pigs, cows and horses. The horses were sold in the Horse Fair which is now High Street. The sheep were put in pens of hurdles, cows and pigs in Angel Pub yard which is now a Bank [Nat West – Ed.].

'We had a Fair in the streets on the first and second Monday and Tuesday in October. It had up and down horses with a good organ, Coconut stalls, Swings and real donkeys which you could have rides on. They sold squibs of water which the boys bought, then chased the girls and poured it down their necks.

'During the war we had Home Guard, Fire Watchers, Land Army Girls, Ranger Guides, Girl Guides, Brownies and Cubs, a Social Club, British Legion Club, a parcel carrier between Woodstock and Oxford and two laundries where the women did the washing in their own homes, then took it back to the people in large wicker baskets.'

Albert Hollis, born in 1936, describes his childhood move from a small cottage at the bottom of the Glyme valley where Brookside Court flats now stand, to the relative luxury of the council houses at Hensington Close, then known as Klondike Close because it was built on the allotments. The road had no tarmac. There was one water pump for every four houses, electricity only on the ground floor and no drain. The 'Piano Cart' or 'honey bucket' collected night soil twice a week from the majority of Woodstock houses until 1953 when the town's sewage system was completed. In the town centre the more fortunate dwellings had drains leading into fissures in the underlying limestone called lissoms. These received the more unsavoury products of the inhabitants and wafted them off through 'caverns measureless to man'. Pot-holing in Woodstock was not to be encouraged. Albert's father drove a coal delivery cart. At the end of the rounds he would permit his small son to take the three Shire horses from the railway station goods yard down to their meadow in Banbury Road on his own, riding one of them bareback. Health and safety was not yet an issue.

SLUM CLEARANCE

One thinks of slum clearance as an initiative for large grimy industrial towns. However the Ministry of Health which supervised and paid for this activity demanded several slum replacement projects in Woodstock. One such was the clearance of a group of cottages in Rectory Lane close to the old Police Station, now Bowley House. Five old cottages housing thirty six persons shared between them three water taps, two drains for water and four earth closets. Washing was strung across the lane for want of any space in a back yard. The owner bitterly objected to the condemnation and busily re-let properties whenever they became vacant. The five shillings a week rents were her only income. Eventually the tenants were re-housed in eight new 'cottages for persons of the working class' built by Woodstock Borough Council in 1938. The site cost £240 with a total building tender of £2966 13s 0d. The Ministry of Health was '*very reluctant because the tender was so high.*' It had a point. At that time a very decent house could be bought for £400.

WOODSTOCK AT WAR

In 1904 fifteen local men of the mounted yeomanry, the Queen's Own Oxfordshire Hussars, returned from the Boer War and received silver tankards from the Duke of Marlborough. Church bells were rung, the band played, the streets were decorated and schools granted a holiday. The funeral of George Hewlett in 1922 reminded the town of an earlier age. The Parish News tells that he was '*one who had served his country well, who had fought not in recent battles but in the Indian Mutiny and in the Crimean Expedition. The incidents of those days may be fading from ones memory but they were times which made full demands on English courage and steadfastness and in*

Oxfordshire Yeomanry Hospital Corps – South African Campaign

which, as in our own day, we had reason to be thankful for many Providential deliverances.'

WORLD WAR I

As in so many places, the World Wars took a terrible toll on Woodstock which, in 1938, was a community of only 1600 people in 409 households. Forty-four men died on service in the 1914–1918 war and sixteen in 1939–1945. The surviving written record of World War I is less detailed than that of World War II. Every street would have been affected by these losses. The individuality of these deaths can be represented by the 1921 funeral of Walter Jack Morley, son of a blacksmith and brother of Robin Morley, the Woodstock chemist whose son Nigel died aged 19 in 1943 as a pilot in the RAF. Walter *'had served in Egypt, Gallipoli and Palestine ... and returned from the war wounded and broken in health to die at home'.*

We do know that during World War I older schoolgirls were required to work as dairymaids at the Blenheim cow yards and eggs were regularly donated to military hospitals in the area. We can only guess at the heroic deed commemorated by the Borough Council's ownership of a German machine gun in 1920. All we have is a letter from the Police Superintendent advising that it would not need a gun licence.

We list below the forty-four men who were recorded on Woodstock war memorial at the end of World War I. It shows how severely the whole community was affected. The personal details which Pat Crutch has collected give some insight into the affected families.

Much of the information comes from the War Graves Commission.

Ernest Ashford: son of Thomas Ashford, stationmaster at Woodstock, died 1917.

Godfrey Ballard: son of Adolphus Ballard, town clerk of Woodstock., died 1915.

Frederick Broadis: of Old Woodstock, died 1918.

Charles Brooks: only son of Charles, a Woodstock glover, died 1918.

Charles Clarke: elder son of William Poore Clarke, ironmonger, Woodstock, died 1915.

Frederick Crutch: younger son of William Henry Crutch, glover, of Old Woodstock, died 1916.

William Crutch: elder brother of the above, died 1919 and buried in Hensington Road Cemetery.

Arthur Davenport: not positively traced, died in action 1918.

Albert Farley: eldest son of James, painter, died 1917.

George Fisher: fourth of five sons of Charles Fisher of New Road, Woodstock, died 1918.

Frederick George Franklin: son of Charles of Brook Hill, Woodstock, died 1918.

George Freeman: born Woodstock, elder son of William, labourer, of Wolvercote, died 1917.

Percival Freeman: brother of above, died 1918.

Charles Richard Guy: born Essex, resident in Woodstock, died 1915.

William Hall: eldest son of Edwin, baker, of Woodstock, died 1917.

Charles Hardy: eldest son of John, carpenter, of Woodstock, died 1914.

Joseph Hawkins: living in Old Woodstock, died 1914.

Hugh Edward Haynes: son of Charles, died 1917.

Herbert Josiah Hine: second of four sons of Josiah, clerk, died 1918.

Clifford Kilby: eldest son of George, of Old Woodstock, died 1917.

Israel Langdon: born Somerset, resident in Woodstock, died 1920.

Alfred Morgan: born Old Woodstock, died 1917.

James Morgan: born Shropshire, resident in Woodstock, died 1917.

War Memorial in the Remembrance Garden

Walter Jack Morley: second of four sons of Frederick, blacksmith, died 1921.

John Painting: born Woodstock, son of George of Old Woodstock, died 1917.

Charles Paisley: born Woodstock, second son of Alexander, draper, of Wishaw House, Woodstock, died 1917.

George Partlett: born Northleigh, died 1915.

Edwin Pittick: not named on the Memorial, received the Distinguished Service Medal in 1915.

Richard Remnant: born Surrey, resident in Woodstock, post office clerk, died 1915.

Ernest Rose: born Woodstock, youngest child of Amos, carpenter, died 1917.

Alfred Slade: born Woodstock, younger son of William, labourer (deceased), died 1918.

Arthur Slade: brother of the above, died 1918.

Charles Smith: born Woodstock, youngest son of William of The Pitchen, died 1915.

Joseph Stephens: born Cumberland, resident in Woodstock, died 1918.

William Stroud: of Old Woodstock eldest son of Frederick, bricklayer, died 1917.

Frederick Stroud: brother of the above, third son of Frederick, year of death unrecorded.

Edward Styles: of Old Woodstock, son of Thomas, labourer, died 1914.

HB Taylor (possibly Herbert Brotherton Taylor): born Old Woodstock, resident in Headington, Oxford, died 1918.

Sidney Taylor: resident of Woodstock, father of six children, died 1915.

Bertram Vokins: born Chelsea, son of George, died 1917.

Robert Whitlock: born Woodstock, youngest of six sons of John, glover, died 1918, received Military Medal.

Ernest Wilkins: not positively identified, probably married Edith M Berry (nurse) in Woodstock in 1911, died 1916.

Percy Williams: born Old Woodstock, son of Thomas, box maker, died 1916.

Albert Willis: fishmonger of Old Woodstock, only son of James, labourer, died 1917.

Alfred Winning: born Woodstock, twin son of Albert, journeyman blacksmith, died 1917.

WORLD WAR II

Evacuees. World War II was declared on 3rd September 1939. One hundred and thirty unaccompanied children and their ten teachers had arrived at Woodstock Town Hall on September 1st and a further 101 smaller children with fifty-one mothers arrived two days later. All were escorted to previously identified billets in private houses by local members of the Women's Volunteer Service (WVS) with a can of meat, two cans of milk one of which was sweetened, a pound of biscuits and half a pound of chocolate.

Three hundred and twenty blankets were hurriedly purchased from Earlys of Witney costing between 16s and 24s 9d a pair.

Many of the evacuees returned home within a few months but in March 1941 there were 524 temporary residents in Woodstock. They were listed as:–

Billeted	250
In houses acquired by the Council	23
Estimate of persons who found private accommodation	200
Government Staff	50

'Government Staff' were MI5 officers (amongst them John Betjeman) working in the Palace and in huts on the forecourt, keeping their eyes on British communists.

Dealing with evacuees who usually came from areas of greater poverty was not easy. Some hosts were quite unused to caring for children. Nobody wanted the bed-wetters in this pre-washing machine era. The billeting was theoretically voluntary so unwelcome children were moved whenever possible. One host owned a sweet shop and was terrified that the children would steal her sweets unless constantly watched. Another wrote *'Please remove Bernard. He has already fell in the brook three times.'* Mrs D-H in Park Street complained that the children allocated to her were too much work for her housekeeper and her maid. What was really behind the statement *'I am unable to keep the girls as I am under the doctor'*? An evacuee woman appalled her landlady by continuing her ancient profession which involved frequent trips into the Park and a queue of American soldiers at the door. On the other side of the coin one mother who came to visit her children found them locked out of the house until the owner returned from work and was justifiably unhappy that their socks were not darned.

Wartime Recycling. We may think recycling is new but Borough records show that in April 1940 Woodstock residents collected paper, brass, copper, aluminium, iron, lead, bottles, rubber, kitchen waste (pig swill), bones, condemned meat, hair, rags and farming string. Scouts and Guides collected the waste paper and there was one salvage volunteer for each street. With echoes of *Dad's Army* a vote of thanks was recorded to Mr Robinson the butcher for the loan of his pony and trap presumably to collect the materials together. Similarly, in 1943 a company of Royal Engineers billeted in the New Road Drill Hall were thanked for the loan of their steam roller to crush old tin cans. The severed stumps of railings outside the Methodist Church today are witness to the fourteen and a half tons of iron collected from there and elsewhere in 1943 to build ships and tanks.

Everything collected was sold and the proceeds were given to good causes such as Spitfire funds (which paid for fighters by public fundraising), the British Red Cross and Mrs Winston Churchill's Aid to Russia Fund.

Woodstock's British Restaurant aka The Welcome Rest. Winston Churchill, that master of words, changed the name of the proposed Government feeding centres to 'British Restaurants'. Woodstock's version was set up in Atherton and Clothier's glove factory on the site now occupied by 58 Oxford Street and Glover Mews. It was operated by the Women's Volunteer Service (WVS) led by Mary, Duchess of Marlborough and her cook. Initially there were fifteen volunteers and four paid staff. We can perhaps spot the influence of Her Grace when we read in the accounts that equipment to start the restaurant included utensils from Selfridges and American cloth from Harrods. Local rumour had it that the Duchess had to be taught how to wash up. This is probably untrue since she herself always washed the priceless Marlborough porcelain once a year.

By 1941 four thousand meals a month were served but the voluntary input gradually weakened until by December 1945 there were eight paid staff and only one volunteer.

In June 1946, 10,926 meals were served costing from one shilling to 1s 4d for adults and fourpence for children. By now the restaurant was largely a school meals service delivering not only in Woodstock but to surrounding village schools. One who ate there as a boy remembers '*ghastly greasy meals mainly composed of root vegetables*.'

War dead in World War II. The toll of World War II was not as great in numbers of Woodstock men – and they were all men – lost as in World War I but the losses were nevertheless significant for a small town and affected several families bereaved by war only twenty years previously.

WJ Batt: records not found.

William Brooks served in Royal Scots Fusiliers, son of Herbert Brooks of Woodstock, died 1944 aged 19.

William James Charlett: served in REME, husband of Cecile Charlett of Woodstock, died 1944 and buried in Hensington Road Cemetery.

Ernest Crutch: served in Oxford & Bucks Light Infantry, son of James & Ismay Crutch, husband of Mabel Crutch, died 1943.

Henry George Freeman: served in Oxford & Bucks Light Infantry, died 1940.

Ronald Hoare: served in Royal Navy, son of Walter (deceased) and Milly Hoare of Woodstock, died in 1940 aged 16 and buried in Hensington Road Cemetery.

Arthur Lacey: Flying Officer in RAF Volunteer Reserve, died 1945.

Frederick Mills: served in *HMS Acasta*, Royal Navy, husband of Elsie Mills of Old Woodstock, died 1940.

John Morgan: served in Royal Engineers, son of Henry & Charlotte Morgan, husband of Elsie Morgan of Old Woodstock, died 1942 at El Alamein.

Nigel John Morley: pilot in RAF Volunteer Reserve, son of Robin and Mary Morley of Woodstock, died 1943 aged 19.

Cyril Morris: served in Royal Engineers, son of Alfred and Lizzie Morris and husband of Alexina Morris of Old Woodstock, died 1944 and buried in Hensington Road Cemetery.

Edward Moss: served in *HMA Glowworm* Royal Navy, son of Henry and Winifred Moss of Woodstock, died 1940.

James Murton: served Airborne Battalion Oxford & Bucks Light Infantry, son of Harry and Lucy Murton, died 1945 aged 25.

Albert Parsons: served in Royal Warwickshire Regiment, son of George and Alice Parsons of Old Woodstock, died 1940 aged 29.

Edward Raymond Turrill: served as air gunner in RAF Volunteer Reserve, son of Ralph and Kathleen Turrill of Woodstock, died 1944, aged 22 and buried in Hensington Road Cemetery.

Reginald Warwick: served as Lance Corporal Royal Armoured Corps, husband of Christina Warwick of Woodstock, died 1944.

WOODSTOCK BOROUGH

New Woodstock had been an independent unit of local government since 1453. At the start of the 20th century Adolphus Ballard, a local solicitor, was Town Clerk and ran the town from his own home in Oxford Street, writing his letters by hand. Responsibilities of the Borough Council gradually increased in complexity taking in highways (on 3rd September 1939 the Borough Council approved the route for a Woodstock by-pass which has never been built), sewers, council housing, civil defence, planning permission, building regulations, public health (e.g. hygiene in local restaurants), refuse collection and disposal, street cleaning and the letting of the Town Hall assembly room where the most profitable tenant was the magistrates' court. During World War II added responsibilities included billeting evacuees and rationing milk and coal.

By 1970 there was a full-time town clerk, a borough surveyor-cum-public health inspector, a book keeper, two dustmen, two street cleaners-cum-handymen, a foreman and various other part-time staff. The Mayor and Aldermen sat in scarlet robes, the councillors in dark blue gowns with bicorn hats. Female councillors were allowed to wear black velvet caps as favoured by Henry VIII. All this was for a population of approximately two thousand. Banbury Road, Shipton Road and several other streets including the Hensington Gate Estate were in Hensington Without parish and paid their rates to Chipping Norton Rural District Council. Then in April 1974 Woodstock Borough was united with four other small authorities to create West Oxfordshire District Council.

The new Parish Council called Woodstock Town Council was responsible for the Town Hall, Community Centre, cemeteries and playgrounds as well as the water meadows gifted by the young Henry VI. The Council gained ownership of the Post Office block and the shops at 2 & 4 Market Street which had been built on the site of the old Guildhall by claiming these as part of the town's ancient heritage. For many years rent from these properties allowed the town to charge a lower council tax than any comparable parish in the county.

THE RAILWAY

Woodstock Railway company was set up in 1888 and chaired by the Eighth Duke on whose land the line ran the four miles to Kidlington station. The Great Western Railway (GWR) operated the trains from the opening in

The 'Fair Rosamund' which conveyed Queen Victoria from Oxford during her visit to Woodstock in 1896

1890 and took over ownership of the single track in 1897. At the time of writing (but not for much longer) the metal plaques inset into the pavement indicating GWR land are still visible outside the old railway station building in Oxford Road. Queen Victoria came on the train to Woodstock in 1896 drawn by an engine named Fair Rosamund after the mistress of Henry II. Was Her Majesty amused? We do not know.

In the line's heyday around 1910 there were ten trips both to and from Woodstock daily, some stopping at Kidlington but others running through to Oxford. The frequency of services and the number of passengers carried gradually declined and the line closed in 1954 long before Dr Beeching's 'rationalisations'.

BLENHEIM PALACE AND THE DUKES OF MARLBOROUGH IN THE 20TH CENTURY

The year 1900 saw Blenheim in the guardianship of Charles, the Ninth Duke and Consuelo née Vanderbilt who was the second successive American heiress to marry into the Spencer-Churchill family and to contribute to the restoration of a fortune depleted by the Fifth, Seventh and Eighth Dukes. The Ninth Duke is best remembered for the installation of the great Willis organ in the Long Library and for his creation of the Italian garden on the east side of the palace and the water gardens which stretch down from the Long Library towards the lake. He was a close friend of his cousin Winston Churchill.

In the early 20th century the huge staff at Blenheim included the butler and housekeeper, several powdered footmen, six housemaids, five laundry maids and a French chef with four assistants in the kitchen. Outside were gatekeepers, gardeners, grooms, coachmen, gamekeepers and the workers on the Park Farm including milkmaids and dairymaid. During World War I the Long Library was a hospital ward with fifty beds.

When the Tenth Duke succeeded in 1934 the staff still included four footmen and two 'oddmen' who were maintenance and handymen. All would have been on their toes when a house party in 1936 included the new King Edward VIII, the American Mrs Wallis Simpson and her accommodating husband. Three years later the Palace was preparing for war. The following instructions were given for action in case of an air raid:

'In the event of hostile aircraft approaching this neighbourhood the police will ring the Palace direct. Anybody taking the message will immediately ring the servants' dinner bell. Everybody is advised to get into the basement and remain there until the all clear is given ...'

The Water Gardens created by the Ninth Duke on the west side of the Palace

The Duke gave permission for the ARP (Air Raid Precautions) and the St John ambulances to practise driving in the dark around the Park. Mr Sacre, the Duke's agent, wrote that he hoped that they would not be too late as the lodge keepers liked to go to bed and would have to close the gates. He also hoped that they would not run into any sheep or cattle. Mr Sacre carefully ordered special gas masks for all the children in the lodges and cottages but forgot to include his own five-year-old son.

The Duchess wished to join the ARP and would not be fobbed off with being guided towards first aid for women. She asked for details of the ARP training. The agent wrote that '*She considers there are instances where women will be just as useful as Wardens. She has already attended a number of lectures in London*'.

A disturbing outbreak of glass destruction at the Blenheim greenhouses was eventually diagnosed as the result of lumps of mud falling from the wheels of Anson aircraft being used for pilot training at Kidlington. The commanding Group Captain was unsympathetic.

In 1940 a regiment of French Canadian troops, the Royal 22nd called 'The Van Doos', were encamped in the park. Local legend has it that they included soldiers of Native American descent who rustled and ate some of His Grace's cattle. A Woodstock policeman, Constable Clifford, told his son that they buried the bones but left the horns exposed to facilitate the release of the animals' spirits and were thereby discovered.

During World War II the Palace was first occupied by Malvern School. The Long Library was filled with beds again. Then MI5, the British Council and the Ministry of Supply followed each other as tenants of the Palace. By the end of the war the Palace was in a poor state. The Tenth Duke opened the Palace to the public in 1950 at half a crown each to pay for the start of a huge forty-year programme of repairs which needed to deal urgently with seven acres of leaking roof. For years the scaffolding never went away but simply moved from one wing to another. Understandably craving some privacy, the Duke created the shaded garden among the trees to the east of the cricket pitch on the south lawn.

The Tenth Duke was proud to have been Mayor of Woodstock from 1937 to 1941, during which time he appeared as the First Duke in a week-long Blenheim pageant which raised money to build The Marlborough School, Woodstock's Secondary School. The Duke was followed as Mayor from 1946 to 1951 by the commanding figure of his Duchess, Chief Commandant of the ATS (Auxiliary Territorial Service) from 1938 until 1940 when pregnancy halted her career.

SIR WINSTON CHURCHILL KG, OM, CH

In 1951 Sir Winston wrote of Blenheim and Woodstock:

'This great house is one of the precious links which join us to our famous past, which is also the history of the English speaking peoples on whose unity the future of the free world depends. I am proud to be born at Blenheim and to be an Honorary Freeman of Woodstock'.

Winston was born to Lord and Lady Randolph Churchill, somewhat earlier than anticipated, at Blenheim Palace in 1874. Baby clothes were hurriedly borrowed from friends of the infant's father in Park Street. If Winston's cousin, the Ninth Duke had been childless, Winston would have inherited Blenheim. He was the heir to the estate between the death of Lord Randolph in 1895 and the birth of the Tenth Duke in 1897. Throughout his life Churchill was a frequent visitor to Blenheim, coming first as a child and, later, to Territorial Army camps in the Park as one of the Queen's Own Oxfordshire Hussars in which he was an active officer for

1947 Mary, Duchess of Marlborough, as Mayor of Woodstock, conferred the Honorary Freedom of Woodstock on Mr. Churchill

over twenty years. He proposed to Clementine and was accepted in the Temple of Diana in the gardens of Blenheim. He also came when he was writing his eulogistic four-volume life of the First Duke of Marlborough between the wars. Sir Winston Churchill was immensely proud of his descent from the First Duke and saw it as his destiny to be the second member of the family to save the country from great peril.

In 1947 Mary, Duchess of Marlborough, as Mayor of Woodstock, conferred the Honorary Freedom of Woodstock on Mr Churchill. At an open air ceremony on Market Place the Borough Council passed a resolution that he was to be '*admitted as an Honorary Freeman in undying recognition of the glory he has shed on this the place of his birth by his services to his country in whom, at the hour of her darkest danger, he lit the flame that led to her victory.*'

Sir Winston's family burial at Bladon by Albert Jerrams, the Woodstock builder and undertaker, placed him in a simple village churchyard near the centre of the land he saved but he would have seen that burial close to his ancestors would underline the significance of his illustrious descent. He could have chosen his spot in St Paul's Cathedral on level terms with Nelson and Wellington. Instead he chose to be close to John Churchill, the First Duke.

9

The Development of the Natural History of the Park

GAVIN BIRD · SHEILA BUDDEN · PAT CRUTCH

A LARGE part of Blenheim – previously Woodstock – Park is a designated Site of Special Scientific Interest (SSSI). Much of this area of the Park has remained relatively unchanged since before the Norman Conquest. Other areas of the park reflect the local geology in a ground flora which ranges from bracken heath to damp acidic grassland with local areas of calcareous grassland. These habitats are also national priorities for nature conservation.

Most of the Park lies on white limestone and forest marble. The south-west High Park is fringed with lower cornbrash but at its highest points is Oxford clay from the Upper Jurassic period. This area remains largely broad leafed woodland. The northern limestone-dominated Great Park is and always has been the chief area for cultivation of cereals whereas the Glyme valley south of this was meadowland.

WOODLAND

The Park contains one of the finest areas of ancient oak-dominated pasture woodland in the country. Secondary ancient woodland – areas continuously wooded since at least before 1600 – is associated with specific communities of plant which thrive in the shady conditions. Plants acting as ancient woodland indicators include wood anemone, wood sorrel, yellow archangel and primrose together with trees and shrubs such as field maple and the wild service tree. Many indicator species are recorded within the Park. Ancient oaks, like all oaks, are home to an enormous variety of insects and fungi and provide nesting and feeding sites for owls, woodpeckers, tree creepers and nuthatches as well as food for a myriad other species.

Ancient oak in High Park

No oak tree in the Park has stood throughout the nine hundred years since Henry I first walled the Park but some of the stag-headed oak pollards probably grew from the acorns of oaks recorded in the Domesday Book. One such parent oak, respected for its great age, was lost at the time of the Civil War. The Parliamentarian Commissioners, in a fit of pique, cut down (according to Plot) *'the Ancient Standard in the high-Park, known of all by the name of the King's Oak, which (that nothing might remain there for the name of the King affixed to it) they digged up by the Roots'*. It was this oak which, chopped into logs, was moved at night apparently by the Just Devil (see Chapter 4) in the dining room of the old Manor House which the Commissioners had turned into a '*Wood-house*'.

High Park reflects ancient forest in being a mixture of dense woodland with areas of wood pasture. In the past, bracken and grassland in such areas were grazed by livestock which helped keep them clear of large trees. Trees in the forest spread from ancient trees to young naturally regenerated saplings which, with dead and decaying wood, support an invertebrate fauna including three beetles listed in the British Red Data Book of Invertebrates, the book which documents rare and threatened species in desperate need of conservation. Another notable invertebrate presence in the Park, not associated with trees, is the Roman snail.

The Park woodland, even though ancient, does not all date from prehistoric times. The Romans cleared substantial areas and may have been the first to modify the natural woodland to a significant extent. The indigenous people were probably also clearing and farming land but there is no evidence of prehistoric settlement in the present forested areas of the Park. (Roman settlements in the area are discussed in Chapter 1). Following the Roman withdrawal most of the cleared land was no longer farmed. Weeds and low growing species such as bramble re-colonised the fields and ash and native shrubs grew up creating cover for small mammals and birds. In wetter areas, such as along the Glyme valley, willows colonised or, more likely, continued to grow on the river banks. Over time, species such as beech and oak would again have become dominant, shading out the light to form dense woodland but encouraging other fauna. Acorns are a delicacy for deer, wild boar, red squirrel and jays. Beech nuts attract finches and other ground-feeding birds. Dead leaves create a thick litter layer where fungi break down dead wood and encourage insect life. Badgers and foxes would have shared the nutrition of the forest with domestic pigs and poultry.

Forest Law controlled activities in the royal forests from Anglo Saxon times until the 19th century when it was disbanded. It burdened local people by prohibiting or limiting many activities within forests. Its main purpose was to protect the woodland for deer and thus for hunting although woodland was valuable for all sorts of reasons and the king presumably needed wood just as much as the local population. Assarting, that is clearing the woodland so as to use the land as pasture, was one largely forbidden activity since it destroyed the habitat for the deer if carried out indiscriminately. Forest Law, which could impose horrific penalties for those caught breaking it, was said to be at its maximum strictness during the reign of Henry II *'an indefatigable hunter'*. Nevertheless some seem to have been happy to pay fines in order to add new land to that which they already farmed. The king's foresters supervised deliberately planned clearing and may have turned the occasional blind eye to others' activities in the forest or alternatively used the Law to extort money out of ordinary people.

Roman Snails still found in the Park

The forest was important to the local people. Their homesteads were, initially at least, fairly temporary buildings so they could move as the agricultural possibilities of an area were expended. For them forests provided wood for fuel, home construction, implements, weapons and protection. For all, wood was the only fuel for heating and cooking. The people in the villages surrounding the park had rights to collect fallen timber for firewood known as

Local residents collecting firewood for cooking and heating

'estovers'. Other rights were 'turbary' or the cutting of turfs for firing and 'pannage' or allowing domestic pigs to feed in woodland. Forest Law forbade allowing animals to graze in areas earmarked for timber production. Over the years many oaks were felled to meet demands for building construction. In the resulting clearings ash and smaller native trees such as hazel and field maple grew and could be coppiced or cut to ground level every ten to twenty years. Coppicing provided a continuous supply of wood for logs and poles. Pollarding willows, that is reducing their height to six to ten feet, encouraged new young growth out of the reach of grazing animals. Willow was the main sources for basketry but ash also supplied strong, pliable, wood for tougher purposes such as fencing or the wattle for 'wattle and daub' houses. The willows in the town water meadows were still pollarded and the branches auctioned for hurdle making into the 1930s. Most native trees can be coppiced and, away from grazing animals, live to great ages forming huge boles covered with mosses and ferns. Elms were not widespread until planted as boundary markers at the 18th century enclosures. Even so, many villages had a 'great elm' on the village green and early 17th century Woodstock documents describe 'Robin Hood's Elm' in Oxford Street. At the end of the 19th century there were two elms: one at the junction of High Street and Oxford St and another, felled about 1890, at the junction of Market Street and Oxford Street.

DEER

Fallow deer thrived in the wooded habitat of Wychwood and the Park. By AD 800 when the Anglo Saxons were dominant in the country, the region provided good hunting for their noblemen. Management of the woodland began. Once the Park was enclosed, the denser undergrowth was thinned out as an effect of grazing by the confined animals. Small clearings created by fallen trees provided space and light for finer grasses and flowering plants such as primrose and foxglove. Later these clearings were fenced around and coppiced. The Anglo Saxon kings probably had some barrier marking and protecting the area around their hunting lodge at Wodestoch so as both to confine the game and to deny entry to poachers and predators. Wolves would have preyed on the game and probably roamed in the Park since they were hunted in the county until the 13th century. By the 13th century raising deer for the hunt and for meat had become a prime function of the Park. The inhabitants of nearby villages were required to provide labour in return for common rights.

Documents from this period record that the nobility hunted hare, hart, buck, roe, wild boar, fox, badger, woodcock, wild cat, marten, otter and wolf. With the exception of wild cat, known only from Iron Age deposits, all these mammals have been found in the Blenheim Park area. In the mid 14th century wild boar were kept in the Park and there was also a falconry.

Deer hunting continued until the end of the 17th century. The Tudor monarchs visited the Park less often than their predecessors but Henry VIII and Elizabeth I are known to have hunted there. Sir Henry Lee, as agent to Elizabeth I, introduced red deer, an unpopular move with local residents who saw their crops damaged. These may have been the species which fled the area in the severe drought of 1605, grazing near the river as far downstream as Richmond Park. The Stuart kings, James I and Charles I, were keen hunters. Following the disturbances of the Civil War ending in the siege of Woodstock Manor House the Park fell into a neglected state and hunting as a royal sport waned. Nettles, thistles and dock would have taken root. Not surprisingly, the unkempt

19th-century 'Robin Hood's Elm' in Oxford Street, Woodstock

appearance of the Park encouraged the unofficial removal of timber and game poaching. Nevertheless, in 1649 there were said to be 1,000 deer in the park. Charles II took little personal interest in hunting at his royal estate and management was left to the Fleetwood family, who maintained a pack of hounds for a later Sir Henry Lee. Lord Lovelace introduced horse racing to the park to raise some revenue, with the first meeting taking place in 1676. Field Trials were advertised at Race Meetings in 1681 and 1692 *'there will be a stag turned out into the country out of Woodstock Park to be run by Hounds'.*

OTHER PARK FAUNA

Most rulers from Henry I to Charles I visited Woodstock regularly. They enlarged the Manor House to accommodate great gatherings for state occasions. Large quantities of food would have been needed along with stabling for horses. Cattle and sheep were raised within the park and pigs and poultry were housed near the King's Houses. There must have been fences or walls to separate domestic and wild animals within the Park. Plough oxen may have been used on a small area of ridge and furrow near Fisheries Cottage. Earlier, there were farms providing cereals and hay in the outlying area.

Rabbits, valued for providing both meat and fur, were brought into the country by the Normans and were soon introduced into royal reserves. Rabbits graze the turf closely encouraging the growth of wild flowers such as harebell, rock rose, salad burnet and bird's-foot trefoil which are features of the grassland associated with the underlying limestone. The present day Park has traces of the artificial warrens or pillow mounds where the rabbits were bred. A 14th-century illustration shows King John riding in the hunt with his dogs creating a picture of what riding through the Park might have been like. Rabbits peep out of their burrows as he rides by.

The Hundred Rolls of 1279 state that the king held fishponds both inside and outside the Park (in Woodstock's meadows). These were created to provide a year round supply of fish, including eel and pike, for the royal table and were regularly re-stocked. *'Lo, the rich pike to entertain your guests, Smokes on the board, and decks a royal feast'* (Vaniere, *Praedicum rusticum*). Bream were brought into the ponds from other royal parks and, along with fish such as tench and perch, are still found in Blenheim's lake today. The concentration of fish attracted otters which were treated as vermin in those times and other fish predators notably kingfishers and herons. It is likely that frogs flourished in the marshy conditions associated with the river and ponds, providing another food source for the herons.

MEADOWLAND

Initially there were royal meadows both within the Park and outside across the Oxford – Chipping Norton road. Those outside the Park known as Le Pool were granted to Woodstock citizens by Henry VI and remain within the possession of Woodstock today as the town water meadows. In 1331 a keeper of the meadows was appointed to manage what were by then well-established agricultural areas. The meadows were probably cut once for hay and then grazed by cattle. Hay was vitally important as winter fodder. The single cut followed by grazing encouraged a range of fine grasses, devil's-bit scabious, yellow rattle, lady's smock and greater burnet whilst orange tip, marbled white and meadow brown butterflies also flourished.

The Whitton family, successors to George Whitton who had been appointed in 1550 as 'controller of the king's buildings and works, overseer and forester of the Parks, Woods and Underwoods', lost the post of controller of the royal manor but remained in the Park as keepers, farming the land and making their own alterations to the Park before and after the Civil War. Around 1700, William Whitton, the last of the family to reside there, listed his meadows as:

- Mill Med under Rose Hill (Mill meadow under Rose Hill)
- Ye hopeward (possibly the hopyard planted by George Whitton in the 1570s)
- Flage mor (Flaggy moor – a field in Old Woodstock?)
- Poge hille (Podge Hill in Old Woodstock park possibly named after the Pod family of later 13th century)
- Ye medow under Quine poll (meadow under Queen Pool)
- Swill med and ye medow under Lettill parke ('Swill' mead and the meadow under Little Park)
- Mere more (Mere moor)
- Rosamonds mede (Rosamund's meadow)
- Eight Ekers hunbora Come and Bladen Coybury (Eight acres Hanborough Combe and Bladon ??Cornbury or coneyburrow – a rabbit warren near Combe Gate)
- Thisel ham (Thistle ham)
- the lore mede (Lower meadow).

These names coincide with those recorded in an official survey of the whole manor made in 1705 when it was handed to the Duke of Marlborough.

The scenic value of the park itself seems to have been of little importance to royal visitors although a gardener for the manor grounds was employed in the late 13th century at twopence a day. Herb gardens growing lavender, mint, thyme, rosemary and chives, feverfew and yarrow were valued for culinary and medicinal purposes. The herbs would have attracted butterflies and other insects. The orchard of pear trees planted at Fair Rosamund's well and the traditional management regime of the orchard would all attract a range of animals and birds including bullfinches which feed on the flower buds. All this formal gardening must have been damaged and decayed by the 18th century when the Churchills arrived.

BLENHEIM

General plans. Laying out the gardens and Park began in 1705 along with building Blenheim Palace. Much of the Park was retained as a deer park, particularly the ancient woodland of High Park in the south-west. In 1781 there were over 3,000 deer. By 1867 there were 770 fallow and sixty-four red deer in the Park but they had been reintroduced for decorative purposes. Blenheim remained a deer park until World War I.

By 1707, some 1,600 elms were established in the two avenues and other plantations. The southern park combined preserved forest trees with new plantings in avenues and circuses.

The great avenue running north from the bridge comprised double ranks of elms centred on a great ellipse. It was fairly complete in 1789 but was reduced to a few scattered clumps by the mid 19th century. Replanting with a double row of elms began in 1896 and in 1902 a more elaborate design was developed with multiple rows of trees and a diamond-shaped centrepiece on the site of the former ellipse. After destruction by Dutch elm disease in the 1970s the avenue was replanted with a mixture of lime and plane trees.

Changes to the river and lake. The earliest plans for the Park included schemes to canalise the river Glyme, inserting rectangular and polygonal basins with islands. In 1722 the duchess engaged William Townsend and Bartholomew Peisley to finish the bridge and build canals to a revised design by the engineer Colonel John Armstrong. Later, under Capability Brown's direction, the great lake was created obliterating Armstrong's

Queen Elizabeth's Island with Woodstock skyline in the background

canals and the existing lake by damming the southern valley at the point where the canalised river turned sharply eastwards. Queen Elizabeth's Island, created when the new lake filled, was planted with trees at an early stage. When the lake's water level fell after dredging in the late 19th century the island increased in size. Below the cascade further canalisation of the river was possible when the Duke acquired the north part (The Lince) of Bladon parish in 1767 thus bringing the whole of the lower Glyme into the Park. The river was widened, deepened, and in places re-channelled and dammed by a long side-cut embankment near Lince Bridge. Below Sir William Chambers' New Bridge the river was widened into a lake before circling the wooded Lince and falling over another cascade into the river Evenlode.

Under the Fourth Duke and Capability Brown the whole length of the valley's rim from the forecourt to the Triumphal Arch was reshaped to provide a view of the water from the Palace. The Great Avenue, the Mall, the radiating avenues in Lower Park and the ancient woodland of High Park were preserved, although some felling probably took place to create vistas. Plantations in the northern Park were preserved and others were added, notably Fourteen Acre Clump and clumps in the valleys north of the lake. The most intensive planting was along the lake where the shape and texture of surviving clumps are still apparent.

In the later 18th century the northern Park was farmed chiefly from buildings at Furze Platt. The farmland was mostly pasture but more land was ploughed in the early 19th century when a large piece of land was added to the north-west corner. The area around Furze Platt in the north-east had already been turned to agriculture by the mid 18th century. Park Farm included not only farm buildings but a menagerie for exotic birds and beasts, including tigers. It was rebuilt and enlarged in the mid 19th century. The painting of the Fourth Duke's tiger by Stubbs still hangs in the Palace.

Later changes. After inheriting Blenheim in 1892 the Ninth Duke dredged the lake and transformed the Park and gardens. He planted nearly half a million trees around the Park between 1893 and 1919. The most notable clumps from that time are on the east side of the river below New Bridge; in the valleys north of Fisheries Cottage; towards Combe Gate; and on the high ground of the northern Park.

Large areas of the Park were converted temporarily to arable during World War I and much of both the northern and southern Park was later turned to arable rotation land. Largely treeless pasture in the south-eastern Park was preserved for a stud farm established at the Cowyards by the Eleventh Duke. From the 1950s onwards there was extensive planting of conifers for commercial purposes to add to the large areas of woodland maintained for game. Following the overwhelming destruction of elms by Dutch elm disease and beeches by beech bark disease in the 1970s a long-term plan was devised to balance the varied and sometimes conflicting uses of the park whilst still conserving or restoring the chief elements of its historic landscape.

FLORA AND FAUNA IN THE MODERN PARK

For many years the lakes at Blenheim represented the largest water body in Oxfordshire. The site's importance for bird life – particularly breeding and wintering wildfowl – has been appreciated by bird watchers who made regular counts through the 20th century to the present day. When new lakes were later created in the county at Farmoor reservoir and other waterbodies established as a consequence of gravel extraction, concerns were raised that Blenheim might become less popular for birds. Some losses have been seen in the numbers of wigeon, little grebe and mallard, the latter having sometimes numbered over a thousand in a single count. The most impressive bird development associated with the lakes is

Lambs in the Park pastures

Snow Geese feeding near Blenheim Lake

growth in the number of gadwalls since the 1950s. Winter counts are now over 150 birds, making the Blenheim population one percent of the total British wintering population.

In this century, faithful birds such as grebes and coots have remained, new species have moved in and some birds that were previously uncommon or rare are now common. Such birds include several varieties of gull, cormorants, common terns as well as greylag, Canada and snow geese. The island supports a grey heron colony, one of a limited number in the county. Herons were previously noted to have last bred at Blenheim in 1784. Their return in 2001 to establish a new heronry on Queen Elizabeth's Island was a welcome development. Historic evidence suggests that the Column of Victory at Blenheim provided the last site of a raven's nest in Oxfordshire in 1843. It is interesting that some of the first ravens to return to Oxfordshire in recent years have been seen at Blenheim.

Inevitably flora and fauna change as the use of the Park changes. The vast numbers of visitors must have some impact. Blenheim is a working estate and a business and as such must make money. Managing such a large area raises many practical problems and conflicting interests. Conservation of the unique natural history of the Park has to be within its modern context. The maintenance of a large part of the Park for pheasant shooting conserves the habitat for many other species. However large areas of the Park remain virtually free of visitors and the interventions of other people are, in many areas, infrequent so traditional species will flourish if the land is sensitively managed. This should ensure continuity of those species which have lived in the area for thousands of years and even promote the return of species which have vanished during periods of neglect.

10 *The Demesne Villages Around the Park*

JOHN BANBURY · PAT CRUTCH

THROUGHOUT this book there have been many references to the demesnes villages (Bladon, Hanborough, Combe, Stonesfield, Hordley, Wootton, and Old Woodstock). The term demesne comes from the Latin *dominicus* – belonging to the lord. It has a special meaning when related to the Domesday survey in that the demesne villages were in the king's possession at the time of the Domesday survey and were also owned by Edward the Confessor.

The Domesday Book of 1086 records that *'in Scothorne, Stauuorde, Wodestoch, Cornberie, Hochenuuode, are demesne forests of the King'*. When William the Conqueror divided up all the land he had taken, he retained royal hunting parks such as Woodstock, where Alfred the Great had a lodge, but distributed the rest to his nobles and supporters from Normandy and to religious foundations. The Domesday Book records estates for taxation purposes in 'hides'. The term was used under the Viking's Danegeld to levy tax and continued under the Normans as the area of land able to support a family or one beast. A hide was of variable size but generally accepted as around 120 acres to a hide. A 'hundred' was an administrative area of a hundred hides. Wootton Hundred, bounded by the Rivers Thames and Windrush to the south but extending north towards Banbury, was the hundred encompassing the Royal Park and the demesne villages we describe.

Adolphus Ballard, Town Clerk of Woodstock in late Victorian times, researched the very early history of the villages, all of which were ancient manors in Wootton Hundred. Their possession by the king in the eleventh and twelfth centuries was by no means complete or continuous. The Bishop of Bayeux held land in Bladon, for which he received payment.

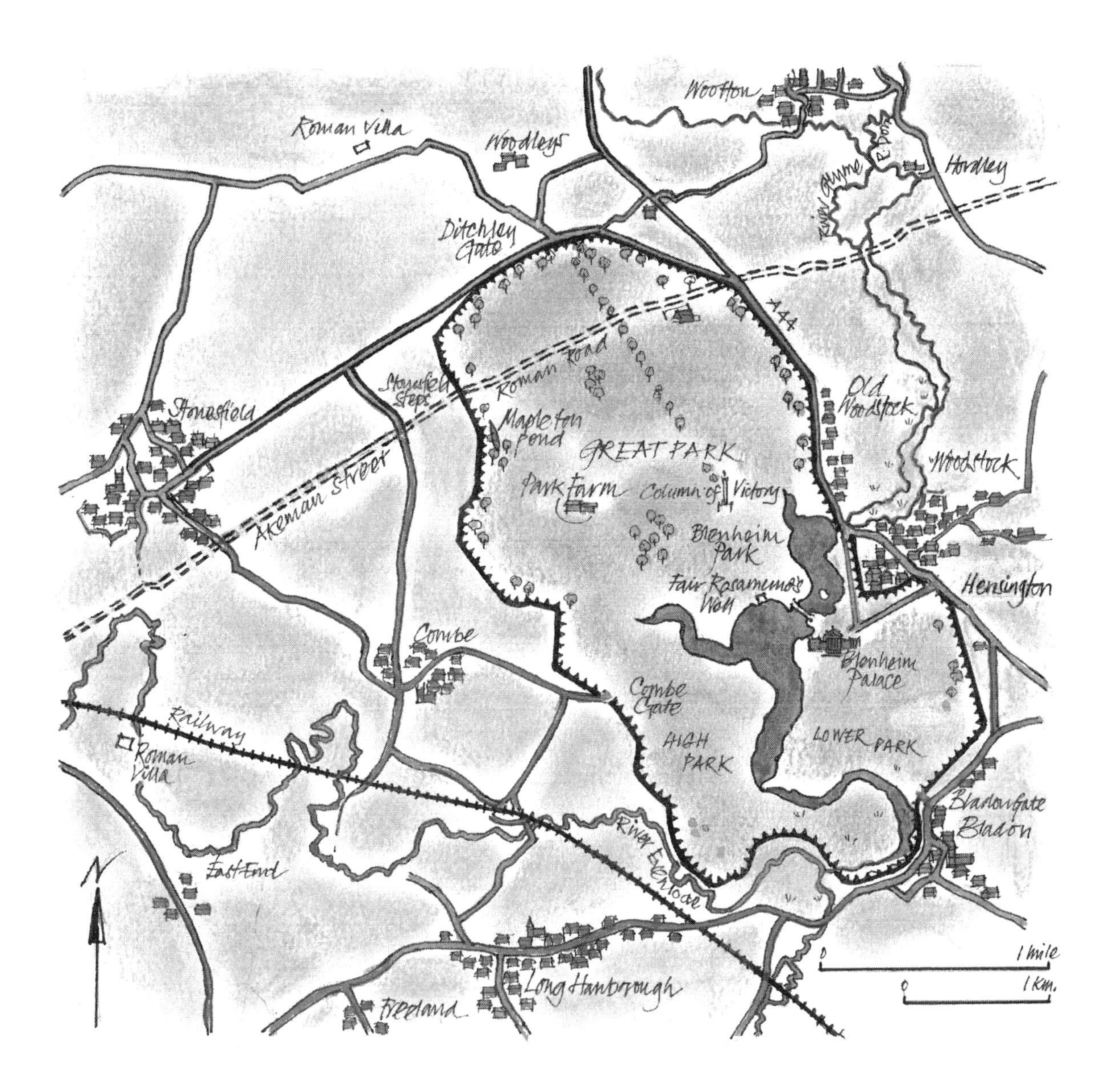

Map 6 The Demesne Villages Around the Park
Bladon, Hensington, Hanborough, Combe, Stonesfield, Hordley, Wootton and Old Woodstock

Roger d'Ivry, Ansger and others held part of Hansitone (Hensington). In early 1200s Walter de Hauville, keeper of the king's birds, held Bladon but on his death in 1219 the king took back the land. Hanborough, recognised even in those days as two hamlets, was taken over by Henry I. Combe was in the king's hands by 1086 although previously another possession of the Bishop of Bayeux. Hordley was certainly held by Edward I in 1275 as he granted Hordley to the parson of Wootton church for ten years for an annual sum of £8 13s 4d. Wootton itself does not come into the king's possession until 1233. The foundation of Woodstock – Old and New – has been described in Chapters 1 and 2.

In 1300 the Great Perambulation (which defined the extent of forests, reducing many to their size under Henry II) included Wychwood Forest and its surrounding area. All the villages mentioned above were recorded as the 'demesne' of the king even though the paragraph above indicates this was not strictly accurate. We are probably dealing with a politically correct description.

BLADON & HENSINGTON

The Manors of Bladon and Hensington share a long history and one that is difficult to disentangle. A round castle on Bladon's southern boundary may, like Grim's Ditch in the north of the Park, have been part of the defences of indigenous people against the Romans. Both manors are ancient inhabited areas of woodland, furze and scrub and were part of Wychwood Forest at the time before 1100 when the Forest reached as far east as Tackley.

Hensington was bounded on the north by Akeman Street and on the west by the river Enis, now the Glyme. It extended east to Tackley, Weaveley and Shipton-on-Cherwell. Bladon (called after the river Bladene, now the Evenlode, which runs past the parish) extended east to Kidlington, south and west to Begbroke, Cassington and Hanborough.

In more recent times, Bladon, Hensington and New Woodstock were all within the ecclesiastical jurisdiction of Bladon and the parish church of St Martin. New Woodstock's chantries and later chapel of ease, developed into Woodstock's church of St. Mary Magdalene but remained part of Bladon parish. It is only in the twenty-first century that the parish of Bladon *cum* Woodstock linked up with several other parishes to become the Blenheim Benefice.

HENSINGTON MANOR

In 1110 Hensington was cut off from Wychwood Forest by the stone walling of Woodstock Royal Park. Henry II made further changes to the manor by exchanging royal land at Hordley for 51 acres of waste land in Hensington on which New Woodstock was built (p. 20). Later annexations into the Park, particularly land just north of Bladon village (The Lince), reduced the width of Hensington Manor further.

At the time of the Domesday survey, Bishop Odo de Tolent owned a large amount of land in 'Hensintone'. None was owned by the King. During Stephen's reign, gifts from the Bishop '*... to God and St. Mary and to the soldiers of the Temple of Solomon*' and from other noble landowners resulted in the Knights Templar possessing large swathes of land in Hensington. Henry II's exchange of land at Hordley Hill for the waste ground outside the Park was thus a negotiation with the Knights Templar. Following the dissolution of the Order in 1312 this Knights Templar land was transferred to the Knights Hospitallers. This created problems later when the Hospitallers demanded the return of 'their' land from New Woodstock together with the corn crop just harvested. The townspeople protested to King John that King Stephen had given them the land free of taxes and fees and that the claim was spurious. The matter was discussed in

Hensington House built in the late 18th century

documents for some time without apparent conclusion. Woodstock continued as before.

Hensingrove, a southern part of the manor, was an area of woodland and scrub which, from its name, may have been used to hunt wildfowl inhabiting the underbrush. Land to the north was probably used to grow grain and peas and for pasture. Sheep are not recorded but may have grazed as they did in Wootton parish. Two chapels, sites unknown, were recorded in Hensington.

The two most memorable buildings in Hensington were constructed in the late 18th and 19th centuries on land owned by the Dukes of Marlborough. Hensington House was built for the Duke's agent opposite the Hensington Gate to the Park. This large house with steps up to a porticoed facade and extensive grounds was demolished between the Wars and replaced by housing along Oxford Road and by the Woodstock Bowls and Tennis Club.

The other major building in Hensington was Woodstock Poor Law Union Workhouse (p. 89), built on land purchased from the Duke of Marlborough. This housed the poor of many parishes and was furnished with a chapel and a hospital, Glyme View, for the sick and elderly poor. It was run by a Board of Guardians and supported from parish rates. Confusingly, the Workhouse called itself 'Hensington House' after the original Hensington House was demolished.

The Marlboroughs also built alms houses, now called Caroline Court, for Blenheim pensioners; the County Police Station; and the railway terminal for the Blenheim and Woodstock branch line. This old station building is now scheduled for demolition and redevelopment. Next door to the station '*Woodstock National Schools erected by public subscription*' is carved on the wall of the original primary school (also on Blenheim land) which had separate classrooms for boys and girls. Between 1968 and 1985 children were gradually transferred to the new Primary School in Shipton Road after which the school was sold as a private house. The senior children went on to the Marlborough School, built in 1939 on Shipton Road, which now has one thousand pupils and continues to expand its buildings.

The civic boundary changed to accommodate the spread of the population from Woodstock Borough down Hensington Road and New Road. Two parishes were created. Hensington Within, bounded by Green Lane to the north and east and the bounds of the old Hensington House grounds to the south, was incorporated into the Borough of Woodstock in the late 19th century. The larger parish, Hensington Without, had its own parish council with elected councillors and clerk until 1985 when the parish council was dissolved. Administration passed to Woodstock Town Council, formed in April 1974 as successor to the Borough Council.

BLADON

The round fort mentioned earlier did not become part of this small settlement outside the Park. In 1086 Bladene was held by Adam, Bishop of Bayeux. The size of his estate was 5 hides, or about 600 acres. The church of St. Martin in Bladon may date from as early as 1200 since an old engraving showed a Norman doorway which was probably removed when the church was rebuilt by the Duke of Marlborough in 1804. In 1659 the Hensington aisle was built on to the north side of the chancel and used for interments of the Napper or Napier family, owners of the chief estate in Hensington. The graveyard was used by Bladon, Hensington and Woodstock until St Mary's Woodstock consecrated its own graveyard.

After the church was rebuilt in 1804, many of the Spencer Churchill family were buried there although the 1st Duke and Duchess are interred in the chapel at the Palace. The most notable grave is that of Sir Winston Churchill, born at Blenheim, who was buried at Bladon in January 1965 with great ceremony following a state funeral in London.

Bladon looking south from Blenheim Park with the tower of St Martin

In Victorian times Bladon had six shops and several public houses. Sadly, as in so many villages, all have now closed except the White House public house and a tea-room with antiques.

COMBE OR COMBE LONGA

Combe lies to the west of the Park, north of the river Evenlode. A piece of gold-plated ring-money and some Roman coinage found there suggest an ancient settlement. In the time of Edward the Confessor it was held by Alwin and Alga but was given to William's half brother, Bishop Odo of Bayeux at the Conquest. It was taxed at one hide. Combe later expanded to some 500 acres and in the mid-12th century increased to 800 acres after assarting (extensive clearing) woodland in the Wychwood Forest and bringing unused land into use. The residents of Combe had their duties under various forms of tenure. Domesday says that *'six villeins with six bordars have three teams'*, meaning that the twelve principle sub-tenants could provide 24 oxen (three teams of eight) to plough the demesne land. A servile tenant had to pay rent of 7s 6d and provide a total of twenty days work for the Manor each autumn. Lower down the scale, a servile cottager would have to pay 2s 9d and work every Friday from 1st August to Michaelmas (September 29th) or pay sixpence rent and work every Monday throughout the year. Over time, if they could afford to, tenants could commute some duties by paying more rent. The population of Combe also had to clean the privies at Woodstock Manor after each royal visit.

The original village of Combe was next to the River Evenlode but, for reasons unknown, was rebuilt further up the hillside around 1350. There may have been a small settlement already where Combe Longa is now but the church, dedicated to St Lawrence, was only built in 1395. Early Norman features suggest that stones brought from an old church in the valley were used in its construction. Much of the early glass has been lost but there are still some well preserved medieval wall-paintings. From 1478 Combe Church was in the gift of Lincoln College and Combe House was used for the vicar as the Rector of Lincoln lived in Oxford. The Rector was expected to pay a supervisory visit twice a year. Between 1820 and 1822 a conflict of views between Rector Tatham and the vicar, Reverend Lee, ended in a riot which only narrowly avoided bloodshed. .

Combe's population remained small with only seventy-two inhabitants in 1537. In the 1700s numbers began to improve and by 1800 the population was 564. The construction of Blenheim Palace and other developments in

Combe village looking across the cricket pitch

the Park together with alternative work created by the industrial revolution may have helped. Certainly fewer people were working in agriculture and over half the population were involved in crafts, trade or one of the three public houses of which 'The Cock' on the green is the only one left.

As in all the local villages, dissenters held meetings in private houses and when they had the resources they built their own chapels. In 1732 John Wesley visited the church as the Lent preacher and was well received. Three chapels were eventually built in Combe but all are now closed. The Reading Room, built in 1891 by Miss Adela Brooke, who let the village use her library at Combe House, survives and among other activities provides visitors with fine cream teas on summer Sundays for the benefit of the Church. She built her Combe Coffee Tavern on the village green, despite some opposition from villagers, to provide recreation indoors to complement that provided by the well-respected Combe cricket team out of doors.

Combe remained without direct road communication to any large centre until the 18th century when the roads between Combe, Woodstock and Long Hanborough were built on land given by the Duke of Marlborough. These became highways following the Inclosure Acts of the 18th century and the turnpiking of the Woodstock to Great Rollright Road in 1830.

Agriculture was always strong in Combe. Most of the land is now owned by the Duke of Marlborough and is farmed by tenants. The Green family came as tenants to Combe early in the 1900s. First farming a few

Combe Mill today

acres of Blenheim land, they now have 3,500 acres under cultivation. Geoff Green recalls that his father bought sheep at a sale in Marlborough one day in the 1930s. The next day the sheep were delivered by train (LMS) to Bletchington Station and he went alone to collect them. He drove them back that evening on foot to Akeman Street Farm at Combe via Stratford Bridge, a journey of over six miles without traffic. Now there are no sheep, beef cattle nor milking herds in Combe.

When the village moved, Combe Mill remained beside the Evenlode. Although initially a corn mill, it became the Blenheim Estate's workshops and saw-mill in 1851. It was a major employer of labour from Long Hanborough. The large steam-operated beam engine, built in 1852, could supply more power than the water-driven mill wheel when the water was low. It has been renovated by a group of enthusiasts who now run the engine in steam for education and entertainment some summer weekends.

HANBOROUGH

The old spellings of this ancient community vary from 'Haneberge' in the Domesday book, 'Hageneberge' in the Pipe Rolls in 1159 and variously Hanborough and Handborough in the Eynsham Cartulary 1268 to 1281. Spelling often depended on the hearing of the clerk who was recording verbatim the details of a piece of land. Sir Henry Lee, Ranger of Woodstock Park under Queen Elizabeth I, refers to it as Hamborrowe and the Post Office and the Railway chose to spell it 'Handborough'. Correct spelling is without the 'd'. There are two hamlets: Church Hanborough is on high ground a mile east of Long Hanborough which is so called because it was far from the church, not because it stretched along the Bladon-Witney road.

An Iron Age settlement on the south side of the River Evenlode and many artefacts and fossil bones uncovered by cultivation and quarrying show that man has influenced Hanborough's character for several thousand years. Before the Norman Conquest it was owned by a Dane called Tonna who held it at a value of nine hides (around 1000 acres). In 1066 the land, held by Gilbert de Gand, had been increased to about 1440 acres by assarting giving taxable value of £10.

By 1172 the manor of Hanborough was held by Henry II, who donated the church to Reading Abbey. The manor was then held by Henry's wife Queen Eleanor until her death in 1281 when the land returned to the king until granted to the First Duke of Marlborough 420 years later. Built with stones from a quarry at Pinsley Wood and some way from the river, the church has both Norman and Early English architectural styles and many interesting features added over the centuries. Its early 15th century octagonal spire makes a fine landmark.

The Octagonal Spire in Church Hanborough

Hanborough's population was about 155 in 1066, rose to 260 in 1481 and then remained at much the same number until the early 1700s. Local serfs each had to give twenty-one days per year for duties on demesne land which included ploughing three times a year, harrowing twice after seeding, mowing for two days, loading hay, carrying four loads of hay and reaping for three days with two men. When necessary they had to work every day throughout the year except Saturdays and feast days but with rents reduced from five shillings to two shillings. The cottagers still had to cultivate and crop their own tenanted land and make enough to pay the rent and *'keep the King's prison in Handborough.'*

In the early eighteenth century Long Hanborough provided travellers with a choice of at least four inns which would have benefited from increased trade with the development of Blenheim. By 1851 the village population was 1150 but it remained principally a farming community with its

The George & Dragon Inn on the main road through Hanborough

own craftsmen, quarrymen, smiths and those sewing gloves from Woodstock. However the wider world opened up when the Great Western Railway built the Oxford to Worcester line in the 1850s providing a station at Long Hanborough with direct access to London. Two motor coach operators, Ernest Oliver and Owen Slatter, also provided transport to hire which facilitated the expansion in outings and seaside holidays between the wars. Today both garages still operate.

The railway suffered many changes of ownership and service, but avoided Dr. Beeching's axe in the 1960s. There is now considerable interest in doubling the largely single track Cotswold line to improve services to Oxford and Worcester and commuting to and from London.

Next to the railway station is the Oxford Bus Museum, created and maintained as a tourist attraction by a group of dedicated volunteers. This incorporates the collection of vehicles and historical records from William Morris (Lord Nuffield)'s motor factory at Cowley. Robert Buckingham, whose family sold Morris vehicles in Summertown Oxford from the 1920s, has established a sales department for the local BMW Mini near Hanborough station. The Mini is now produced in Cowley on the site of the Pressed Steel factory only three quarters of a mile east of where the Morris Mini originated in the spring of 1959.

Three inns were noted in Cassey & Co's 1868 gazetteer. John Fox held the George and Dragon, Thomas Lay had The Swan, and William Henry Lay ran the Three Horseshoes and also dealt in coal. Kelly's Directory of

1931 lists The Bell, The Swan, The Three Horseshoes, The Shepherds Hall Inn, The Hand and Shears, The George and Dragon and John Greenaway as beer retailer. There was also the Bull and Bush during World War II. Today The Hand and Shears Inn at Church Hanborough, The Bell, and The George and Dragon still serve food and drink but many of the local shops and trades listed in 1931 have gone.

STONESFIELD

'*Stonesfield is a village and parish, four miles from Woodstock, in the hundred of Wootton, Woodstock union, and diocese of Oxford. The inhabitants are principally employed in the slate pits, of which there are several in the parish, with extensive under ground works*'. So wrote an unnamed correspondent to a guide in the 1860s, stating the population as 650 and the village 1020 acres of which 300 were woodland.

The community known as Stuntesfelde was recorded in the Domesday Book as having one hide (120 acres) worth thirty shillings and ten square furlongs of woodland in Wychwood Forest, about one and a quarter square miles of land in all. Stonesfield, situated above the north bank of the River Evenlode, is the most distant of the seven demesne vills (small villages) from Woodstock Park. In 1087 Aluric held the land from Robert de

Stonesfield Church today

Stadford (Stafford) but no record is given as to who held it beforehand. He had several sub-tenants of which, for example a vergater (tenant of a 'vergate' or quarter of a hide of land) could be compelled, as in Hensington, to work every day except Saturdays and feast days to be excused three shillings of his rent. Other arrangements could also be made by sub-tenants to reduce or increase their rent by working for more or for fewer days each year although, before 1280, tenants were expected to work for the Lord of the Manor for nothing almost every day of the year. Stonesfield tenants also had land of their own, something not recorded for other villages except Hanborough.

In the 14th century Stonesfield should have paid money in rents to the king as Lord of the Manor of Woodstock for each of its inhabitants on the demesne farm. No rent is recorded. The demesne land had been let at a rack rent of sixpence an acre and returned a higher income to the king than would probably have been achieved if the peasants had been obliged to work for him for nothing. By the mid 16th century the more profitable practice of leasing demesne farms instead of using tenancies and of providing both stock and grain for seeding were widespread.

The village was protected from pressure of development since it was never near a through route and did not suffer from royal visits or later incursions of the Royal Park. Its slate miners were independent, working in their own time and self-employed. When a good frost was expected the church bells called them from their beds to remove the protective turf which kept the quarried 'pendle' stone laid on the fields moist, so that the frost would split the stones into slates. From being one of the poorest communities in Oxfordshire during the middle ages, Stonesfield became relatively affluent. Resident during Victorian times were David Barrett, quarryman, George Howes, Thomas Lawton senior and junior and Caleb Townsend, all slaters and plasterers and skilled at using the riven pendle stone; Albert Oliver, mason and builder; two carriers; and supporting trades. The Black's Head, Maltster and Shovel, Marlborough Arms, Rose and Crown, and White Lion inns provided victualling for villagers and visitors alike. (The Black's Head, the Boot Inn and the White Horse are recorded in 1931). Shopkeepers, including baker and shoemaker, took care of the physical needs whilst the Church of St James (established before 1224), the Wesleyan and Primitive Methodist Chapels looked after their souls – a lively village. Farming was as important as in the other demesne villages but the village income was augmented by women sewing gloves at home and by men working in the slate industry.

Stonesfield has been a source of two sorts of ancient remains, one infinitely more ancient than the other. Dr Plot, first Keeper of the Ashmolean Museum, in his 17th century *Natural History of Oxfordshire* described many fossil shells and an extraordinary large piece of thigh bone from a local quarry. Was this quarry Stonesfield? In the next century three gigantic vertebrae and other pieces of bone from huge animals were retrieved in the Stonesfield mines. These remained only curiosities until they attracted the interest of Buckland who was the first Professor of Geology at Oxford University in the early nineteenth century. Buckland hoped the Stonesfield bones would help him verify the Biblical Flood. The Stonesfield mines descended *'by vertical shafts through a solid rock ... more than 20 feet thick, to the slaty stratum containing these remains'* and the remains were *'absolutely imbedded in the deeply situated stratum'*. The great French scientist Baron Cuvier, on a visit to Britain to review its fossils, pronounced these Stonesfield bones as parts of a massive lizard (*saurus* in Greek). Modern paleontology was born.

The other ancient remains at Stonesfield are those of Roman occupation including a large villa complex with tessellated pavements measuring thirty-five by twenty feet discovered around 1711. Unfortunately the pavement was destroyed by agricultural operations, but not before a resident recorded it as a vast needlework – the Stonesfield Tapestry – now, with other local finds, in the Oxfordshire Museum at Woodstock.

Stonesfield's population was only 374 in 1801 but almost doubled over the next fifty years partly due to the success of the mines. Among the 670 inhabitants noted in the 1851 census were thirty men involved directly with the slate industry, 112 women stitching gloves, 120 agricultural workers who also dug slate part-time and some itinerant railway construction workers. In addition there were all the trades, crafts and shops one would expect to find in a village.

Between 1801 and 1804 the Parliamentary Commissioners effected land inclosures. Those having tenancies or leases were given compensatory plots of land, the Duke being the main holder. The Rector of Stonesfield also received significant compensation for the glebe land. As with all these awards, some people received little or nothing but the end result was a much more productive farm system with land continuously farmed by one occupier instead of a system of small, widely separated field strips whose occupants changed annually.

The basic shape and layout of the village has not changed much since the Middle Ages. Some new buildings – a modern primary school, a village hall, a library and some more modern housing along the north side of the village – have been added and some infilling has taken place. A core of two or three small shops and Post Office provide for the village, which depends these days on work elsewhere, including working from home by way of electronic communication.

HORDLEY

Hordley, possibly named after a long forgotten 'hoard' of Roman coins or jewellery, has always supported the smallest population of the demesne communities. It is three-quarters of a mile south east of Wootton and is first mentioned in 1194 when there is reference to a royal estate and the Sheriff accounted sixty shillings for the farm. There was a chapel by 1286 and over 100 acres under the plough. Much of the land was farmed by residents of other vills such as Weaveley (today only three farms half a mile apart) since there was too much for the few resident land-holders to have ploughed themselves.

By 1243 the demesne farms were let to tenants who collected rents from individual peasants. The total annual rental was £5 14s 2d for the 151 acres. Rack rents of ninepence an acre were paid to the king. The cottagers had to provide services such as mowing, hoeing, reaping, autumn work and threshing sheaves of corn twice a week for the Lord of the Manor in line

Hordley Farm *c.*1900

with those of other demesnes. Hordley's tenants also had to clean the hall and chambers of the King's Houses before and after each royal visit to Woodstock. Using timber from the king's forest, they had to repair Stratford Bridge over the Glyme where Akeman Street still crosses the river. A water mill existed about half a mile up stream from Stratford Bridge on the River Glyme but this ceased action around 1800.

In 1279 Hordley's land area had increased to 325 acres. The 1377 poll tax returns show there were nineteen tenants and in 1524 tax was paid by just five adults. By 1607 only three houses seem to have been occupied with other cottages turned into stables or farm buildings. By the 18th century there was one remaining farm cultivating 300 acres,

The farm was owned by the Gregory family who also farmed at Hanborough. John Hetis held the land in the 1400s and a John Gregory married Maud, Hetis' grand-daughter, and was granted the property which then passed down from father to son for several generations. The farmhouse has architectural components dating from 1500 but later the Gregorys installed wood panelling possibly rescued from the demolished Woodstock Manor House. The ancient farm was sold in 1811 to the Fourth Duke of Marlborough. The bases of old walls and fishponds were still visible near the farmhouse in 1825.

The ornithologist and natural history expert Dr. Bruce Campbell lived at Hordley in the latter half of 20th century. It is to him and his colleagues that we owe the fine record of birds and the natural history of the Glyme valley and Blenheim Park as well as the long term conservation of the Glyme and Dorn valleys which pass through Hordley and Wootton.

Sansoms Farm marks the boundary of Hordley and Hensington at the crossing point of Akeman Street and the ancient green lane linking Woodstock and Barton Abbey.

WOOTTON

Wootton developed as a fairly independent and self-contained village north of the Glyme and up the adjacent slope. In 950 King Edgar, son of Edmund, King of the English, granted 20 hides of land at Wootton to his 'minister' Aethelric. Another estate of five hides was held by the Bishop of Coutance. Before this, Buckinghamshire county records suggest Hordley was held briefly by Walford the White, a thegn (Nobleman) of Queen Edith, a Norse family. But then, William the Conqueror was the grandson of a Viking pirate!

Five hides of Aethelric's holding were taken into Henry II's ownership on the death of Eleanor de Vitry, Countess of Salisbury, in 1233 and both holdings were then combined to form the Manor of Wootton. The profits and taxes were collected by the King's appointed guardians of the Manor of Woodstock. The parish church of St. Mary had an early foundation with architecture of Early English, Decorated and Perpendicular styles and further 'improvements' and additions over the centuries. The late Georgian Rectory is a large house known now as Wootton Place.

Agricultural production has always been the foremost occupation in Wootton. Woodstock Manor Farm was established early on in what is now Old Woodstock which became a separate demesne village in the 16th century so we describe it below. Wootton Parish lost about 51 acres when Old Woodstock separated and was assessed with Woodstock Manor.

Before the separation, the population of Wootton was just over a hundred. In 1279 there were 140 tenants from ninety resident families and 144 adults paying poll tax in 1377. In 1642, probably because of plague and civil disturbances, only ninety-seven men over eighteen years were counted. Population increased in the 18th century probably due to the outworkers who were glove cutters and gloveresses stitching gloves as a cottage industry for the Woodstock trade (no glove factory was established in Wootton), and working on the developing estate at Blenheim. By the mid-19th century the population was 1238 including those living in Old

Wootton viewed from Top Lane looking north *c.*1900

Woodstock and the village was bustling with tradesmen and businesses. There were ten farmers and a bailiff; three inns: the New Inn, the Three Horseshoes and Killingworth Castle; and a *'beer retailer and painter'*. If the latter refers to the King's Head, the term 'painter' is because he could not make enough money as a landlord. In late Victorian times the business of slaughterman was carried on at the King's Head. The list of resident traders and craftsmen included blacksmith, miller, saddler, carpenter and builder, boot and shoe-maker, two shopkeepers and two bakers, corn dealer, tailor, and carrier.

In 1872 Wootton achieved some notoriety because of unrest in the agricultural community. This was exacerbated by poor housing conditions, low wages and the refusal of employers to improve their situation. In the early 1830s, the rector reported to the Poor Law Commissioners that Wootton's labourers earned just about enough to survive. In 1872, the local branch of the National Agricultural Workers Union and the leadership of Wootton Methodist Christopher Holloway inspired 120 farm workers to withdraw their labour and hold large scale demonstrations, demanding a rise in wages from eleven to sixteen shillings a week. Meetings with all the local protesters were held in Combe, Hanborough and Bladon and a few soldiers had to be brought in by Wootton farmers to help with the harvest. The trouble died down as the need for the numbers of workers on farms declined with the introduction of new mechanical farming equipment. At the same time, less work was available to the glove cutters and gloveresses in the village as Woodstock factories were using more stitching machinery.

Between the Wars, most of the trades had declined although there were nine farmers, a blacksmith, boot repairer, butcher, two shopkeepers, carrier and a Post Office still in the village. By 1939 an insurance agent, a midwife and a parish clerk, first appointed in 1894, were also resident. Edith Bloomfield, the midwife, paid a schoolgirl sixpence a week to carry all her water from the village well. Most other needs were covered by travelling salesmen from Woodstock businesses who had regular rounds for clothing, shoes, ironmongery and household goods as well as collecting and delivering for the remaining glove manufacturers. Coal was collected from the coal yards at the Great Western Railway stations and kindling collected from the Park. Mr Judd's garage on the main Oxford to Stratford A34 (now the A44) road by the New Inn dealt with all types of motor repairs and fuel supplies and had a carrier's licence. With the greater use of motor vehicles came the opportunity to move out of agriculture and work away from the village for higher wages. By this time Old Woodstock's

This old cottage in Wootton, dated AD IIII, was located below Balliol Farm opposite the present shop

population was counted separately and, in 1931, Wootton had a population of 548 on an area of land measuring 4,211 acres.

By the 1950s the calm atmosphere of the village and its small stone walled cottages with local slate roofs were attractive to many looking for a quiet life. Undeveloped houses and cottages could be purchased from their owners for modernisation at reasonable prices since, with little profitable work nearby, agricultural workers and their families left their tied cottages. Very soon properties in the village became too costly for local young people to buy. Jobs in Oxford at the large car factories and work in the expanding Cotswold tourist industry made Wootton, like some other demesne villages, into a dormitory community. The resulting loss of local businesses deprived Wootton of its blacksmith, carrier, village shop, post office, butcher, tailor, builder, and others. The Village Shop is now run as a limited company and charity and the whole is co-ordinated by a manager. The old New Inn now named The Duke of Marlborough on the main A44, the modern Oxford to Aberystwyth road, and the Killingworth Castle on the B4027, the old Aberystwyth road, remain.

OLD WOODSTOCK

Old Woodstock is not mentioned in the Domesday Book of 1086. From the accounts of Henry of Huntingdon it is generally agreed that Old Woodstock on its present site originated from clearance of a settlement inside the park inclosure. Initially viewed as part of Wootton, Old Woodstock became a separate demesne of Woodstock Manor in the 16th century. It remained administratively linked to Wootton parish until 1886 when the southern, built up area, was joined to Woodstock municipal borough. Yet, only one hundred years ago quit rents were still being paid for land occupied in Old Woodstock to the Duke of Marlborough as Lord of the Manors of Wootton, Old Woodstock and Hordley.

Once established in Henry I's time as the nearest habitation to the royal Manor, it was the duty of Old Woodstock residents to serve the court when the king visited and for that they were granted common rights. Later, however, King Henry II declared the vill too remote from the Manor and allotted land for building outside the park wall but nearer the Manor House. Thus the settlements became Old and New Woodstock.

There is little documentation for Old Woodstock's earlier times. The 1279 Hundred Rolls list tenants of the King's Woodstock demesne. Henry Pravus or Pranus paid fourpence for a tenement, probably the present Manor Farm previously Praunce's Place. Henry Pod rented ground at the boundary with tenement and piggery. This may refer to the Old

Manor Road Old Woodstock

Woodstock park entrance formerly known as Pod or Podge's gate. In 1361 the View of Frankpledge for Wootton was held at this gate, denoting its position of some importance. The 'View of Frankpledge' was the court hearing at which pleas were heard. It was usually held at the same time as the Sessions for the Peace when fines for misdemeanours and taxes were set and collected from each cottager and tenant. All men were expected to attend and the meetings were usually held in the open, close to a significant local site, often an ancient barrow or mound.

The typical layout of a medieval village was a cluster of houses around the lord's manor with 'closes' along the highway, beyond which lay the common fields. The early settlement of Old Woodstock probably consisted of a few habitations near Manor Farm where the highway was crossed by an older thoroughfare, now Balliol Lane, running east/west. Beyond the farm the lane branches north east and is described as a cart way in the 1770 inclosure awards. It may also have continued due east to link with Hensington across a bridge over the Glyme. Across the field to the north of Barn Piece estate runs a public footpath to Wootton, Wootton Way, which provides a shorter route than the main highway.

Few early references to specific buildings in Old Woodstock exist but one of the earliest recorded buildings was a brewhouse in the possession of the Chantry of St. Margaret of Woodstock sold in 1548 following the Dissolution.

Beginning at the Wootton end of Old Woodstock and moving down the east side of Manor Road, the A44, there was first a series of 'closes'. Spittal House Close, the most northerly and now part of Hill Rise, was possibly associated with a medieval hospital. Cottages on the site were once the Rose & Crown pub owned by the Prior family. Mock Mayor making was held there from the mid-18th century. William Crutch, a fourth generation glover, employed several local men in his leather dressing workshop and drying ground on what was Spittle House Close. Numbers 38 to 44 Hill Rise now occupy the site.

The cottages south of Barn Piece farm are probably the oldest part of the settlement but the farmhouse and some small paddocks are all that remain of the farm itself. St. Andrews Church, built in 1886 on Balliol College land after Old Woodstock was transferred from Wootton Parish, is now a private house. The most significant building is Manor Farm House with its distinctive chimney, a 20th century replica of the 13th century octagonal chimney carved from a single stone. It has been wrongly described as the birthplace of the Black Prince (see p. 28).

Apart from the Black Prince public house on the bank of the river Glyme, Old Woodstock today is entirely residential. The building across the road from the Black Prince is the mill which served Old and New Woodstock and the Manor House from medieval times although the buildings have been rebuilt and altered by successive tenants. It may be the site of one of two mills mentioned in Wootton Hundred in the Domesday Book. The First Duke of Marlborough purchased the mill in 1720 and it continued in use until 1870. The mill wheel was removed in the 1960s to improve the flow of the river but the pumping equipment remains. Nearby, at 5 Manor Road, a plaque identifies the site where George Kempster raised the famous apple, formerly Kempster's Pippin but now the Blenheim Orange Pippin.

Further north, the cottages on 'The Bank' were built at different times and many are Grade II listed. In the 19th century three of these houses were licensed premises for selling beer (there were nine ale houses altogether) and there was a wheelwright's yard. The 'kissing gate' into the park replaced a ladder-and-stile with steps on to the wall and down the other side. Residents with heavy trucks had to load inside the park, unload at the stile, carry wood and truck over the wall, and reload on the outside. The nearby row of cottages numbered 53 to 63 are known as Ladder and Stile Row.

Further up the road was a public house called the Rose and Crown and St Andrew's Square where several small cottages were demolished in the 1950s. Dorothy Calcutt's mother, the subject of *The Salt of The Earth,* was born in one of these cottages. The Infants School built in 1870 at the instigation of Miss Jane D'Oyley, was sold in 1974 as a private house. Miss D'Oyley was a local benefactress, providing food and clothing for the poor of Old Woodstock.

From 1891 the late 18th century Glove House was the factory premises of Frank Bryan & Co, a Worcestershire firm specialising in sports gloves. The manager lived in the house. The factory buildings at the back of the plot housed four or five glove cutters downstairs and a number of female machinists upstairs. Women outworkers did hand and machine stitching and tying. Bryan's closed in 1967. From the yard and barn opposite, the Knibbs family, father and son, ran their carriage service from the yard and barn, firstly with horse drawn transport and later with the brown van familiar in the local area.

The old Gate House, number 131, was the toll house on the turnpike road. The toll gate was moved from the causeway to this position before 1806 to allow residents of Old Woodstock to pass freely into the 'New' town.

The Mock Mayor of Old Woodstock. New Woodstock on the south bank of the River Glyme elected a real mayor from 1453 or earlier. Old Woodstock on the north bank was outside the borough boundary but for many years has elected its own Mock Mayor. In these celebrations it is the Mayor and Council of New Woodstock who are being lampooned. Today, the Black Prince, formerly the Wheatsheaf Inn and recorded in 1775, is the base for the Mock Mayor celebrations. Initially the ceremonies were hosted by the two 'Rose and Crown' inns.

It is not certain when the ceremonies began but the Mock Mayor custom may have begun long before the dates on the old wooden mace which bears the inscription '*This mace was made at the sole expense of Charles Llewellyn Perkins Esq., Mayor of the ancient village of Old Woodstock Anno Domini 1786.*' Mock Mayor Making has lapsed on many occasions. After it lapsed in 1928 it was revived briefly in the 1950s and a further revival by Old Woodstock Football Club in 1984 continues today. Each revival brings its own version of the ceremonies.

In present times a crowd gathers outside the Black Prince. Candidates make extravagant promises as to what they will provide for Old Woodstock, preferably satirising events in New Woodstock. The Committee then announce the pre-arranged winner of the contest which is as fair and democratic as any 18th century election. The Mock Mayor wears a brass chain made up of assorted metal fragments such as curtain rings, an old red blanket and a top hat. He is accompanied by his Town Crier, Mace Bearer, Constable, Drummer, Morris men and Committee. Cine film from 1928 shows the men in bowler hats and the women in academic dress. The ceremony ends with a march and the ritual ducking of the new Mayor in the Glyme to emerge up the steps into the Black Prince garden.

A small handful of other 18th century Mock Mayors survive, one being the Mock Mayor of Ock Street in Abingdon. The Old Woodstock ceremony remains to remind us of the independence of this nine hundred year old community which is today part of the town known generically as Woodstock.

Bibliography

Angerstein R RR. 2001. *Illustrated Travel Diary 1753–1755: industry in England and Wales from a Swedish perspective*, translated by T & P Berg, The Science Museum, London.

Aubrey J. 1696. *Miscellanies upon Various Subjects.* http://www.fullbooks.com//Miscellanies-upon-Various-Subjects2.html accessed 13.01.2010.

Bailey RS, Rector of Hanborough 1911–27. (Undated). *Hanborough.*

Ballard A. 1908. *Woodstock Manor in the Thirteenth Century.* Stuttgart, Kohlhammer.

Ballard A. 1896. *Chronicles of the Royal Borough of Woodstock*. Oxford, Alden & Co.

Banbury Family documents.

Banbury J. 2006. *Fire! Fire! Fire! The History of Woodstock Volunteer Fire Brigade.* Woodstock and Bladon News.

Bapasola J. 1988. *Household Matters, Domestic Service at Blenheim Palace.* Woodstock, Blenheim Palace.

Bapasola J. 2009. *The Finest View in England*. Woodstock, Blenheim Palace.

Barlow F. 2002. *Thomas Becket*. London, Folio Society.

Baxter I, Lenagan I F. 1992. *The Old Woodstock Mayor Making: a History 1782–1992*. http://oldwoodstock-mockmayor.com/8.html accessed 01 03 10.

Blair J, Baxter I. 1992. Praunces Place *Oxfordshire Architectural and Historical Society: Oxoniensia* LVII.

Blair J. 1994. *Anglo Saxon Oxfordshire*. Stroud, Alan Sutton.

Bond J, Tiller K. 1987. *Blenheim : Landscape for a Palace.* Gloucester, Alan Sutton.

Brewer JN. 1813. *Oxfordshire.* London, Vernor, Hood & Sharpe.

Byng J. 1996 (first published 1796). *Rides round Britain*. London, Folio Society.

Cadbury D. 2000. *The Dinosaur Hunters*. London, Fourth Estate.

Calcutt D. 1999. *The Salt of the Earth. Diary of a Poor Family in Woodstock, 1900.* Charlbury, Wychwood Press.

Campbell B. 1964. *Oxford Book of Birds.* Oxford, Oxford University Press.

Cassey E. 1868. *History, Gazetteer and Directory of Berkshire and Oxfordshire.*

Climenson EJ. 1899. *Passages from the Diary of Mrs. Lybbe Powys of Hardwick House, Oxon., A.D. 1756 to 1808* London, Longman & Co.

Corporation of Woodstock. 1951. *Official Guide.* Oxford, Alden Press.

Cozens-Hardy B. 1950. *The Diary of Sylas Neville 1767–1788*. London: Oxford University Press

Crossley A, Townley SC, Colvin C. 1990. *Woodstock*. In Elrington CR (ed) *The Victoria History of the Counties of England. Vol XII Wootton Hundred (South)*. Oxford, Oxford University Press.

Crutch P. 2010. *Close Families of Old Woodstock*. Charlbury, Wychwood Press.

Danbury E. 2007. *World War II*. Woodstock and Bladon News.

Danbury E. 2009. *What I remember of Woodstock*. Woodstock and Bladon News.

Day CJ. *Old Woodstock*. In Elrington CR (ed) *The Victoria History of the Counties of England. Vol XII Wootton Hundred (South)*. Oxford, Oxford University Press.

Defoe D. 1986 (first published 1724). *A Tour through the Whole Island of Great Britain*. London, Penguin Books.

Doran S. 2003. *Elizabeth, Exhibition at the National Maritime Museum*. London, Chatto & Windus.

Doran S. 2009. *Man and Monarch; Henry VIII*. London, British Library.

Eddershaw D. 1995. *The Civil War in Oxfordshire*. Stroud, Alan Sutton.

Elrington CR (ed). 1990. *The Victoria History of the Counties of England. Vol XI Wootton Hundred (North)*. Oxford, Oxford University Press (for Horley, Wootton).

Elrington CR (ed). 1990. *The Victoria History of the Counties of England. Vol XII Wootton Hundred (South)*. Oxford, Oxford University Press (for Bladon, Blenheim, Combe, Hanborough, Hensington, Old Woodstock, Woodstock).

Fiennes C. 1982. *The Illustrated Journeys of Celia Fiennes* c.1682–c.1712. C Morris (ed). London, Webb & Bower.

Fowke R. 2010. *The Real Ancient Mariner*. Bishop's Castle, Travelbrief Publications.

Fowler M. 1989. *Blenheim, Biography of a Palace*. London,Viking Penguin.

Green DB. 1951. *Blenheim Palace*. London, Country Life.

Green DB. 1984. *The Churchills at Blenheim*. London, Constable.

Greenway DE (tr). 2002. *Henry of Huntingdon. The History of the English People, 1000–1154*. Oxford World's Classics. Oxford, Oxford University Press.

Guy J. 1988. *Tudor England*. Oxford, Oxford University Press.

Hibbert C. 1992. *The Story of England*. London, Phaidon.

Hibbert C. 2001. *The Marlboroughs*. London, Viking Penguin..

Hilton L. 2009. *Queens Consort. England's Medieval Queens*. London, Phoenix.

Hoskins WG. 2005. *The Making of the English Landscape*. London, Folio Society.

John Fox. 1563. *Acts and Monuments*.

Kelly's Directory of Berkshire, Bucks & Oxon.

Kielmansegge. 1902. *Diary of a Journey to England in the Years 1761–1762*. Translated by Countess Kielmansegge. London, Longman & Co.

Lingard R. 1973. *The Woodstock Branch*. Oxford, Oxford Publishing Co.

Marshall E. 1873. *Woodstock Manor and its Environs; in Bladon, Hensington, New Woodstock, Blenheim; with later notices*. Oxford, Parker.

Marson CL. 1901. *Hugh, Bishop of Lincoln*. London, Edward Arnold. www.guteberg.org/files/26065/2065-8.txt accessed 12 01 2010
Mavor WF. 1810. *A New Description of Blenheim*. Oxford, J. Munday.
Mortimer I. 2008. *The Perfect King. The Life of Edward III*. London, Vintage.
Mortimer I. 2009. *The Time Traveller's Guide to Medieval England*. London, Vintage Books.
Moul T. 2007. *The Historic Gardens of England*. Stroud, Tempura Publishing.
Neale JE. 2005. (First published 1934). *Elizabeth I*. London, Folio Society.
Neville S.1950. *The Diary of Sylas Neville 1767–1788* ed. Basil Cozens-Hardy. London, Oxford University Press.
North A. 1998. Polished Steel Wares of Woodstock. *Journal of the Antique Metalware Society Vol. 6*
Ordnance Survey 2001. *Roman Britain*. (Fifth edition).
Oxfordshire County Council Heritage Search: Environmental Records.
Oxfordshire County Records. *Inquisition into the Customs of Woodstock Manor*, 1551, translated by Dr Mavor in 1803.
Phair, RW. 2002. William Longespée, Ralph Bigod, and Countess Ida. *The American Genealogist*, 77.
Plot R. 1705. *The Natural History of Oxfordshire* (second edition) Oxford: Brome. Reproduced: USA, Kessinger Publishing.
Powell GH. 1975. *Stonesfield*. Oxford, Truexpress.
Powys L. 1899. *Passages from the Diary of Mrs. Lybbe Powys of Hardwick House, Oxon., A.D. 1756 to 1808* ed. E.J.Climenson. London: Longman & Co.
Rackham O. 1986. *The History of the Countryside*. London, Dent.
Richmond C. 2009. *A collection of records from the parishes of the Woodstock Poor Law Union and Workhouse 1835–1849*. Oxford, Black Sheep.
Roast N. 1975. *The History of the Woodstock National Schools*. No publisher given.
Robb-Smith AHT. Undated, circa 1956. *The Woodstock Chimes*.
Schumer B. 2000. A Brief History of Wychwood before the Enclosures. In Keighley C (ed) *Discovering Wychwood*. Charlbury, Wychwood.
Scott W. 1969 (first published 1826). *Woodstock*. London, Dent.
Shelmerdine JM. 1951. *Introduction to Woodstock*. Woodstock, Samson Press.
Shelvocke G. 1726. *A Voyage round the World by Way of the Great South Sea*. London, J Senex.
Sherwood J, Pevsner N.1974. *The Buildings of England: Oxfordshire*. Harmondsworth, Penguin.
Spokes Symonds A. *Oxfordshire People and the Forgotten War*. Witney, Robert Boyd.
Stevenson J (ed). 1858. *Chronicon Monasterii de Abingdon*. London, Rolls Series.
Surch R, Campbell JM.1982. *An Atlas of Oxfordshire Mammals*. Oxfordshire Museums Occasional Paper No.1. Oxford, Oxford County Council.
Warton T. 1778. *History of English Poetry*. Quoted in Edward Marshall. 1873.

Weir A. 2000. *Eleanor of Aquitaine*. London, Pimlico.

Weir A. 2006. *Isabella. She-Wolf of France, Queen of England*. London, Pimlico.

William of Malmesbury. *Chronicle of the Kings of England*. Oxford, Bodleian Library

Willmot CH. 1979. *The Bells of St Mary's*. Published privately.

Woodstock Borough Archives. Held at Oxfordshire County Record Office, St Luke's Church, Cowley.

Woodward F. 1982. *Oxfordshire Parks*. Oxford, Oxon Museum Series

Young A. 1769. *A Six Weeks Tour through the Southern Counties of England and Wales*. London, W Strachan.

Ziegler P. 1997. *The Black Death*. London, Folio Society.

Acknowledgements

We acknowledge with gratitude the help given by the following:

FOR FINANCIAL SUPPORT:

The Greening Lamborn Trust
The Woodstock Society
West Oxfordshire District Council
Woodstock Special Events Fund
Several private individuals

FOR HELP WITH ACCESSING DOCUMENTS:

English Heritage
Henmans LLP
Oxfordshire County Record Office
Roger Henman
The Banbury Family
The Bodleian Library
Woodstock Town Council

FOR PREPARATION OF ILLUSTRATIONS:

John Leighfield CBE
Robert Wheeler

The sources of our illustrations are acknowledged in the list of illustrations but we recognise particularly:

Her Majesty the Queen
His Grace the Duke of Marlborough
Colonel N. D. Clifford MBE
John Peverel-Cooper
Michael Hallam
John Leighfield CBE
Woodstock Town Council

FOR CHAPTER FOUR:

The Marlborough School

Index

Page numbers in *italic* refer to black and white illustrations

Akeman Street 9, *2*
Alfred the Great 4
Anne, Queen 56, 62
Aquitaine, Eleanor of 17
Armstrong, John 116
Arthur, (Prince Arthur) 35
Aubrey, John 19, 51

Ballard, Adolphus 103, 120
Banbury, C.W. 93
Banbury, John 91, 92
Becket, Thomas à 22, *22*
Beckett, Doug *82*
Bedingfield, Henry 39
Bell founding 72, *75*, *76*
Black Death 30
Bladon 37, 120, 122, 125
Blenheim Palace 60, *106*
Blindheim, battle of 58
Boleyn, Anne 34
Brown, Lancelot (Capability) 14, 60, 67, 69, 117
Bull Inn *38*, *39*

Carnarvon, Earl of 48
Catherine of Aragon 33, 34, 38
Carillon 75, 76
Chamberlyns' Accompts *36*
Chambers, Sir William 69, 90
Chantry school *35*
Charles I 44
Charles II 55, 57
Churchill, Lord Randolph Spencer 87, 107
Churchill, Sir Winston Spencer 87, 102, 105, 107, *108*, 125
Civil War 45
Clarendon, Earl of 53
Clifford, Fair Rosamund *17*, 16–19, 32
Combe 37, 122, 126, *127*
Cornwell, Richard 35
Cromwell, Oliver 48, 51
Cut steel 77–81, *78*, *80*

Defoe, Daniel 70
Domesday Book 16, 29, 120, 123, 141

Edmund of Woodstock 28
Edward I 28
Edward II 28
Edward III 28
Edward IV 30
Edward VI 35, 36
Edward VIII 105
Edward, the Black Prince 28, *29*, 140
Elizabeth I 37–42, 83
Elizabeth II, Her Majesty the Queen 83, *84*
Ethelred II 4, *4*
Evelyn, John 55
Everswell 14, 18

Fair Rosamund, steam locomotive 104, *104*
Fairy Queen 42
Fawcett, Samuel 50
Feast of St Matthew 25
Fell market 81
Fiennes, Celia 55
Fire Brigades 90–93, *92*, *93*
Fishponds 114
Fleetwood, William 50–52
Fletcher's House 92
Foxe, John 40

Gloving 81–85, *82*, 141
Glyme, river 1, 9, 60
Godolphin, Sydney, Earl of 63, 64
Godstow Abbey 18
Green, Geoffrey 128
Grim's Ditch 30
Guildhall 30

Hanborough 37, 128, *129*
Hawksmoor, Nicholas 60, 65
Henry I *10*, 10, 11
Henry II 16–22

Henry III 26
Henry VI 28, 30
Henry VII 32–33
Henry VIII 33–35
Henry of Huntingdon 12
Hensington 122, 123
Hentzner, Paul 40
High Lodge 42, 44, 54, 64
Hiorne, Edmund 46, *46*
Hordley 37, *134*, 134–136
Horse races 55
Hugh, Bishop of Lincoln 23

Isabella, (Queen Isabella) 28

James I 43
James II 56
John, (King John) 26

Keane, Richard and James 72–75
Knights Hospitallers 123
Knights Templar 20, 123

Langspee, William 18
Lee, Sir Henry 41, 43, 113
Lenthall, William, M P 46, *46*
Le Pool 30, 115, 128
London Zoo 11

Malmesbury, William of 16
Malvern School 107
Manor House 14, *14*, *15*, *33*
Margetts, Doug 92
Marlborough, John, First Duke of 57, 60, 62, 108, 141
Marlborough, Fourth Duke of 71, 117
Marlborough, Ninth Duke of 105, 118
Marlborough, Tenth Duke of 105, 107
Marlborough, Eleventh Duke of 118
Marlborough, Mary Duchess of 102, 106, *108*
Marlborough, Sarah, Duchess of 56–67
Mary Tudor, (Queen) 38, 39
Matilda, (Empress) 12, 22
Menagerie 10, *10*
Mock Mayor of Old Woodstock 142

More, Sir Thomas 34

New Woodstock 20

Old Woodstock 1, 37, 139–142

Paris, Matthew 27
Parry, Thomas 39
Philip II, King of Spain 37
Philippa (Queen) 28, 66
Pigs 16
Portmoot Court 30
Praunce's Place 28, *29*

Railway 104
Rainsborough, Colonel 50
Richard I 25
Rochester, John, Earl of 53
Rosamund's well *19*
Round castle 4
Royal 22nd Regiment 106

St Andrew's Square 94
Ship tax *45*
Simpson, Mrs Wallis, see Edward VIII
Slum Clearance 96
Snails, Roman *111*
Stonesfield 37, 131–134

Thomas of Woodstock 29
Tower of London 11
Town Hall 86, 90, *95*

Vanbrugh, John 58–65
Victoria (Queen) 105

Wall 7–9, *8*
Waller, William 48
West Oxfordshire District Council 104
Whetton, Walter 52, 115
William I 5
Woodstock Entertainment 41
Wootton 37, 122, 136–139 *136*
Workhouse *88*, *89*, 124
Wyatt, Sir Thomas 37
Wychwood Forest 1